Endorsements

"Joe Colavito shares a uniquely powerful story that enfolds the greater story of God's love and human worth. The characters are unforgettable and the message is clear and life-changing: what's on the inside really does matter! A must read."

D.B. Shelnutt, Pastor

"Great work, a work of joy and remembrances drawing us all into the place we need to be."

David Cook, author of Golf's Sacred Journey

"We're all just alike. We spend our days chasing our dreams and tracking our outward accomplishments. Jelly Donut Junction is a refreshing reminder that our true value is better measured by what's inside—our character."

Debbie Griffiths, RNC, author of Little Lady, BIG DREAM

jelly donut junction

Wayne –

Embrace ev<u>ery</u> moment !

[signature]

Eph 3:16-19

JOE COLAVITO

jelly donut junction
WHAT'S INSIDE MATTERS

TATE PUBLISHING & *Enterprises*

Published by Tate Publishing & Enterprises, LLC
127 E. Trade Center Terrace | Mustang, Oklahoma 73064 USA
1.888.361.9473 | www.tatepublishing.com

Tate Publishing is committed to excellence in the publishing industry. The company reflects the philosophy established by the founders, based on Psalm 68:11, *"The Lord gave the word and great was the company of those who published it."*

Book design copyright © 2008 by Tate Publishing, LLC. All rights reserved.
Edited by Amanda R. Webb
Cover design by Kellie Southerland
Interior design by Stephanie Woloszyn
Illustration design by Eddie Russel
Author Photo by Karen Burns–www.karenimages.com

Published in the United States of America

ISBN: 978-1-60462-012-6
1. Inspirational: Motivational
2. Religion: Inspirational
08.03.27

Dedication

To our children—Jessie, Courtney, Andrea, Matthew, and Katie.

Always keep seeking your role in *The Story* and loving one another.

In loving memory of Arnold Gardner—February 27, 1959–April 25, 2007

Thank you for showing us how to stand firm when life's unexpected storms appear on the horizon. Your faith and courage were inspiring.

Table of Contents

Author's Note
Hidden in Plain Sight

The Story is unfolding.

If we look closely and listen carefully enough, this becomes clear. Each scene is in motion—filled with new sights and new sounds. And every moment is fresh; no two are alike. As amazing as this is, there is more.

You have a role! Do you see it? Are you excited about it? We all have a role. Are you living yours out? Or are you getting too caught up in the scene to enjoy your role?

Jelly Donut Junction is an allegory written to remind us adults to look at life through the faithful eyes of a child again. It's so easy to lose our perspective. The demands, the harried pace of this world, and our circumstances can blind us to our childlike sense of wonder and rob us of our joy. When this happens, we need to get away—to find a place where we can renew our minds and refresh our souls.

Jelly Donut Junction is such a place. So, today if you're feeling rushed, harried or lost in the scene—or you perceive that you've been miscast or outcast in some way, this book will encourage you to more fully embrace and appreciate your role in *The Story*.

Climb on board as Matty Boy and his Poppa embark on

The Quest of a lifetime; a journey to find the hidden treasure. Join the adventure as their magical day unfolds and a young boy's *questions* pave the way for an unforgettable joyride. Along the way, each of our experiences will be different, but the simple truth that binds us all together will remain the same—*what's inside matters.*

One final thought before we begin. Please don't allow the childlike appearance of *The Story,* the silly names of the characters, or the simplicity of the scenes to distract you from discovering the invaluable life lessons *hidden in plain sight.*

Enjoy your quest…

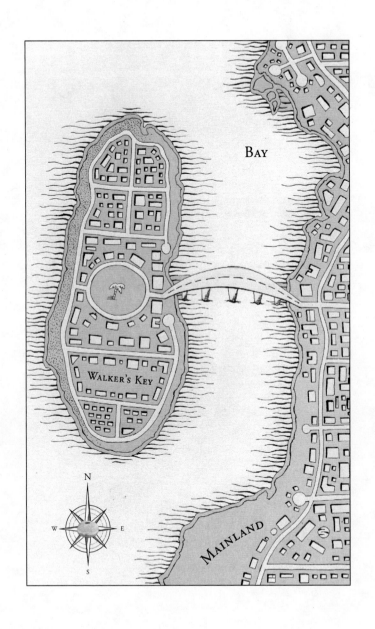

The symbols.

What do they mean? They rattled around in the old man's head as he drove through the night. He had felt the gravity of their meaning since his youth, yet he still didn't know what they meant.

One day I will know. One day. But not this day, he thought to himself.

This day was spoken for already. This day was about his grandson's quest, not his.

The Quest

On the eleventh day of the seventh month of the year, several hours before sunrise, a joyful old man tiptoed into his grandson's bedroom wondering what this day would reveal. As he scooped the boy up, hoping not to wake him, Matty opened his eyes and mumbled, "Poppa, where are you taking me?"

"We're going on a *quest*," whispered the old man.

As he emerged from the contemporary stucco ranch buried amidst dozens of others just like it, the old man headed straight toward the antique pickup truck parked beneath the street light.

"What's a *quest*, Poppa?" asked Matty.

"A quest is like a treasure hunt," he said.

As soon as the words left the old man's mouth, he felt like the world stopped spinning, just for a moment—as if he were standing on the edge of time, straddling the invisible boundary separating the past from the future. *It seemed like only yesterday that my father said exactly the same thing to me,* he thought to himself.

He paused, hoping to regain his perspective. Although the entire scene lasted mere seconds, it was surreal. He pivoted quickly back and forth several times. Every time he looked backward, he saw his son's contemporary home; every time he looked forward, he saw the antique truck he had inherited from his father many years ago.

"What kind of treasure?" His grandson's question snapped the old man out of his trance-like state, calling him instantly back to the present moment.

"Hidden treasure, the kind we were created to seek, the kind that's buried deep inside our hearts. It's the only kind worth chasing, because once we find it, it lasts forever. No other treasure can compare to it."

"Hidden treasure? Awesome, Poppa! Have you ever found it?"

He buckled the boy into the passenger seat, closed the door, and walked around to the driver's side. After slipping into the worn vinyl seat and buckling his own belt, he said, "Oh yes. I've found it. Now I'm looking forward to helping you find it too. Try to get some sleep while I drive us to a very special place—a place where your quest for the hidden treasure will begin."

Before placing his hands on the wheel or turning the key in the ignition, the old man closed his eyes and took a deep breath. He reflected on the fact that—regardless of how much the world changed around him, no matter how different things appeared on the outside—one thing always remained constant and true. *What's inside matters.*

When the old man opened his eyes, he found his grandson already fast asleep. He started the truck, shifted into first gear, and pulled away from the curb. After driving for quite a spell, they reached the bridge connecting the mainland to Walker's Key. The old man still couldn't get used to the new bridge.

Again, he felt he could hear his father's voice; his presence in the truck was palpable. Somewhere, rising from the deep recesses of his soul, he could hear his father whispering the family mantra. *Things aren't always as they appear. The scene—what we can physically see—too often masks the unseen truth about life.* Not a day went by that the old man didn't reflect upon this mantra. It shaped the way he viewed everything.

After spending his entire life in Jelly Donut Junction, the old man and his wife moved to the Midwest to be closer to their son and their only grandson, Matty Boy. Before long they missed the warm weather and convinced their son and his family to move back home. They relocated together to a nice community on the mainland, about ninety miles from Jelly Donut Junction.

While the old man was away, the department of transportation had replaced the original drawbridge. Although he had seen the new bridge several times since moving back to the area, driving down this final stretch of road still surfaced mixed emotions. He could remember, not too long ago, when a simple little bridge led to a remote hideaway. When the moon, the stars, and the single working headlight, on what at the time was his father's pickup truck, provided the only light for miles. *Now look at this place. The hideaway is an overcrowded getaway, and the familiar flat bridge is now an artistic archway reaching up to the heavens. It's really an incredible sight,* the old man thought to himself.

As he approached the apex of the four-lane expanse, he

looked in his rearview mirror. Then, he looked ahead toward Walker's Key. Since there were no other cars coming in either direction, he stopped and turned off his lights. There was barely any change in visibility. Even though it should have been pitch black, given the time of morning, it seemed like midday.

The new bridge didn't have any street lamps. It didn't need them. The entire sky was lit like a giant halo. The artificial light cast from both sides of the bridge appeared to turn the night into day. *What a shame,* he thought. *What other changes have taken place in the past two years? I sure hope they haven't knocked down the old buildings in the circle.*

Despite being disappointed by how many high rises were crammed into so little space, the old man's excitement grew as he approached the traffic circle. The farther he drove into Walker's Key, the less the artificial lights permeated the darkness, so he flipped his headlights back on. For the most part, Jelly Donut Junction still looked the same. Poppa breathed a sigh. *At least they've left the buildings from my childhood days intact.*

As the old man entered the circle, he compared what he was physically seeing to the images stored in his memory bank. Immediately to his right was the children's hospital. As he continued slowly around the circle, he passed the town store. *Imagine that. We used to think that place was a one-stop shop, but that was before Wal-Mart entered the scene.* The headlights cast themselves onto the old barbershop. It still marked the halfway point in the circle, the spot where the town ended and the road leading to the beach began. The old man stopped, rolled down his window, and breathed in the salty air. *Ahhh, there's nothing like the smell of the ocean breeze.*

As he continued driving around the roundabout, he passed the bank that occupied the space between the beach and the traditional-looking wooden billboard. After passing the old billboard, he pulled into the parking lot of the donut shop. He and his grandson had finally reached their destination.

After pulling into the parking lot, the old man glanced into the rearview mirror one last time. The hospital was still visible across the way. And as best he could tell, the park area in the center of the circle had been preserved.

The old man's mind drifted to all the conversations that had taken place underneath his favorite tree. He wondered if the palm tree his older brother had nicknamed Rooty was still standing at the center of the fountain. Unfortunately, despite the assistance from the artificial lights, it was still too dark to tell, but deep down inside, he sensed she was still there.

As he turned off the engine, his heart leapt with anticipation. He felt like a kid again. He sat quietly inside the red truck, looking up at the message on the sign. *After all these years he's still standing in the spotlight,* he thought to himself. As he read the familiar words displayed on the sign's face, the memories of this special place came flooding back. For it was here, as a young boy, that the old man had been given a new lens on life. It was here that he had first experienced a sense of wonder and joy. This was the place where his yearning to live life to the fullest was awakened; the place where his quest began. It was in this very place that the old man discovered his hidden treasure—and first laid eyes on the symbols.

"Wake up, Matty Boy," he said as he gently shook his grandson. "We're here."

Matty's eyelids were heavy. "We're where, Poppa?

"We're in the center of Jelly Donut Junction."

"That's a funny name, Poppa. Why do they call it that?"

This is what the old man loved most about his grandson—his undeniable and unquenchable curiosity. "It's called Jelly Donut Junction because it's the home of the world's best jelly donuts. Want one?"

The instant the old man opened the door to the antique truck, his favorite smell from his childhood, the sweet aroma of homemade donuts, flooded the vehicle. *Wow, some things never change. Boy, those donuts smell great!*

"Poppa, can I have two if I drink my milk all gone?" Not waiting for an answer, Matty unbuckled himself, vaulted out of the truck, and raced toward the front door of the donut shop. He pulled on the door, but it was too heavy for him to open. This forced him to wait for his grandfather, who was doing his best to keep up.

Once inside the doorway, Matty caught his first glimpse of the powdered treasure. He had never seen anything like it—an entire wall full of donuts. For a moment, he froze, his eyes scanning, his mouth watering. The wheels inside his head churned.

"Poppa! Poppa! How many different kinds are there?"

Knowing any answer he provided might derail the boy's quest, Poppa chose to stoke his curiosity instead. "How 'bout we get a whole bunch and let you find out for your-self?

The boy could barely believe his ears. He wrapped his arms around the old man's leg and squeezed. "Poppa, you're the best!"

The old man winked at the woman behind the counter as he ordered. "Miss, please load us up a couple of boxes with one of each kind."

From where the old man stood, the look on the boy's face said it all. Mattie Boy had surely found the hidden treasure; his little mind raced with the excitement. While the woman boxed up the donuts, the boy watched closely to make sure she selected at least one of each kind. Mean-while, the old man admired the antique cash register on the counter. When he was done, he shifted his attention to the two pictures hanging on the wall behind the register.

Although the old man battled to mask his feelings, it was no use. The memories associated with the pictures were too vivid. The emotions they surfaced were too strong to ignore. It was in that moment that the old man realized this day held more in store for him than he'd anticipated. He'd been so focused on guiding his grandson's quest, he had overlooked the impact this day would have on him.

As the first tear escaped and rolled down the old man's cheek, Matty began volleying questions. "Poppa, what's wrong? Why are you sad?" The old man pointed toward the pictures while Matty kept firing away. "Who are they, Poppa? Why are their pictures on the wall? Can you pick me up so I can see?"

"I'm not sad, Matty Boy. These are tears of joy."

"Hey, is that you, Poppa?" Without waiting for a response, he pointed to the larger of the two pictures. "Who is that guy with all the donuts?"

"No, that's not me. That one is the donut man. He opened this place a long time ago, when Poppa was just a little boy like you."

The old man took a deep breath. The entire scene had triggered memories tucked away deep in the archives. For a moment he felt like that little boy again; the one who, on more than one occasion, got caught sneaking a donut. He drifted back into the past, reliving the fond memories of his childhood. As he reflected on the incredible role the two men had played in his life, more tears streamed down his face. No longer could he hold them back.

Matty propelled his grandfather back into the present moment by tugging on his trousers. "Poppa! Poppa! Can we eat our donuts now?"

The woman handed the old man a napkin so he could wipe away his tears. By the time he responded to his grandson, "Sure, go for it," Matty had already pulled one of the boxes off the counter and was making a beeline toward the corner booth.

For the second time that day, the old man felt he was perched on the edge of time. *I'll be darned. I couldn't have scripted it better myself,* thought the old man. *What is it about that corner booth that draws us in?*

To the casual observer, Matty's seating choice would have appeared to be purely coincidental, but not to his Poppa. The old man's quest began years earlier in this very booth.

After placing the other box in front of the boy, the old man slipped into the booth and took a sip of his coffee. He watched as his grandson ripped open the box and grabbed his first donut. Poppa knew from experience that there was no stopping curiosity once it grabbed hold of a young boy's imagination, so he just sat back and watched the show.

Without hesitating, Matty began poking his tiny index finger into one donut after another. And with each passing donut, the old man knew his grandson was inching closer to setting his quest irreversibly in motion—on a collision course with his destiny. Matty was about to step onto a well-worn path; a sacred trail that would lead him directly to the hidden treasure. Unbeknownst to the boy, it was the same path upon which his father and his grandfather had traveled before him.

After poking his finger into several more donuts, the smile on Matty's face faded. He set the donuts down and looked up at his grandfather. The young boy's expression was not surprising; the old man remembered seeing it on his son's face many years ago. The look on his grandson's face was one the old man would never forget; this was a moment he would cherish forever. He could practically hear the boy thinking. Although it was difficult to remain silent, Poppa knew that's exactly what the situation demanded.

A few seconds passed before Matty broke the silence. "Poppa, how come these donuts are all the same kind on the inside?"

What the boy didn't know was that his real quest had now begun. He had just asked the right question, at the right time, to the right person—his Poppa. This was the question the old man had hoped the boy would ask. Answering it was the real reason they had embarked on this treasure hunt to begin with. This was the place. This was the day. The time had come for Poppa to share *The Story*.

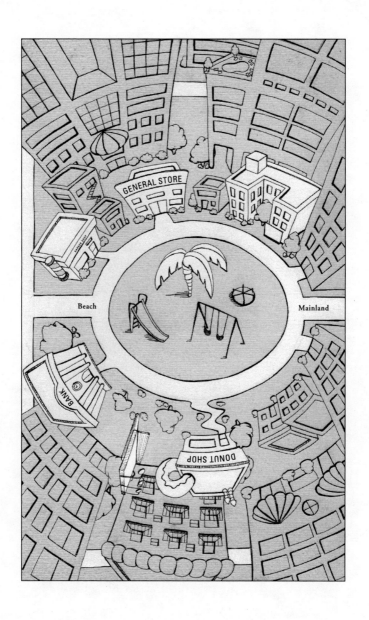

The Story

Once, in an obscure town nicknamed Jelly Donut Junction, four ordinary characters found themselves linked together in the quest of a lifetime. Each sought to understand their role in *The Story*. Each was different from the rest. None were related nor did it look like they had anything in common.

Three of the characters were so ordinary—a palm tree named Rooty, a billboard named Woody, and an old brick building named Wally—that on most days they simply went unnoticed. They appeared to be just an insignificant backdrop, part of a familiar scene in the busy lives of the townspeople...but that was before everything important happened. That was before the three united to serve a common purpose and to teach all of us an invaluable lesson. *Things aren't always as they appear. The scene— what we can physically see—too often masks the unseen truth about life.*

The fourth character was a blind teacher named Danny who loved children, especially the sick ones from the children's hospital near the center of town. He spent his days in the park across from the hospital singing songs, spinning tales, and sharing simple truths about life with the brave little patients and their anxious parents. He encouraged all he met to open the eyes and ears of their hearts. Some did. Some didn't. Those who did found their role in *The Story*—and were changed forever.

○ ○ ○

The setting sun cast the palm tree's shadow diagonally across the large wooden sign's face. Woody welcomed the cool shade. Rooty, on the other hand, enjoyed the much-needed rays on her trunk.

The two were best friends despite their innate differences. Woody had been raised in the lumber yard. Rooty grew up under the artificial lights in the nursery along with the other plants and trees. Woody was inflexible, both physically and in his outlook on life. Rooty was not. She was open to adventure and filled with wonder. Woody preferred the shade, having learned from his parents to avoid overexposure to the Sun. Rooty's mother, on the other hand, had told her daughter amazing stories about the Sun every night before bedtime. She encouraged Rooty to grow closer to the Sun each day and to search for her role in *The Story*.

Rooty loved being planted in the center of the park in the midst of all the activity. She couldn't dream of living in a better place. She was in the perfect position to see everything she wanted to see, except for the Sun. She could watch the people go in and out of Wally's front door, visit with Woody whenever she wanted to, and watch over the children in the park. Despite all that, Rooty was still frustrated by the fact that the high rises around the circle completely blocked her view of the Sun.

It had been nearly three years since the tree doctor drove Rooty from the nursery to the park on his flatbed truck. Unfortunately, because it was dark and overcast that day, she never got to see the Sun. When she awoke the next morning, the Sun was already up. It was then she realized that she was unable to twist far enough to see the Sun when he was rising, and that she was too short to see over the buildings when he was setting. The rest of the time, he was either directly overhead, where her branches blocked her view, hiding behind Wally, or sleeping through the night.

At first, Rooty's frustration with the buildings blocking her view consumed her days, but then instead of letting the high rises bring her spirits down, Rooty began dreaming of the day she would grow tall enough to see over them. Although she cherished the Sun's life-giving rays on her back each morning, she longed to see him for the first time. For now, she could only imagine what he'd look like. She imagined he'd be absolutely amazing.

Woody was a typical sign. He lived to draw attention to himself. After all, that's what signs do, right? They compete for people's attention. Woody specialized in image management, but deep inside, he was very insecure. He worried about losing his position in town. His visibility amongst the townspeople was very important to him.

Some days, Woody felt vulnerable, inadequate, and underappreciated. On those days, he wondered if all the time he invested in seeking people's attention was worth it. This was especially the case when he compared himself to Rooty. He couldn't understand how she could spend her days dancing in the wind, giggling with the geckos, singing with the seagulls, and watching the children. *Doesn't Rooty have something more important to do with her time?* he wondered.

The young palm tree didn't seem to care about how she appeared to others. As far as Woody could tell, managing her image didn't appear to concern Rooty in the least. Neither did having a job or assuming any kind of responsibility at all, for that matter. From Woody's vantage point, all Rooty ever talked about was growing closer to the Sun. She didn't seem to care about anyone or anything else.

Although Woody would never admit it, at times he was jealous of his best friend. That's because even though Rooty made no effort to attract other people's attention, every single tourist seemed to notice her first. It frustrated him when the tourists commented on how adorable she was and stopped to take their picture with her. Nobody ever took their picture with him.

○ ○ ○

As the last traces of sunlight dipped beyond the horizon, the wind began to blow harder. A young boy scampered after his hat, desperately trying to catch up to it as the wind blew it teasingly down the sidewalk. Woody and Rooty overheard the shop owner saying, "The worst is yet to come," as he nailed plywood over the shop's windows.

"What's he doing, Rooty?" asked Woody.

"He's covering the windows of the donut shop."

"Whew. That's a relief." In an attempt to cover his trail, he added, "I mean, it's not like I'm worried about losing my position or anything. I was just curious, that's all."

Over the years, Woody had been repainted so often that he could no longer open his eyelids. They were sealed shut, in effect making him blind. This forced him to rely more upon his hearing and visual updates from Rooty than he ever cared to admit.

"The worst is yet to come. Ha!" interrupted Knotty, Rooty's older cousin, who had been born with a knot on his shoulder. He was as stubborn as a mule. Lately, all he cared about was declaring his independence; proving that he could stand alone.

Knotty twisted his trunk quickly back and forth. He tried intently to break free from his guidelines—the wire cables supporting him. "Rooty, once I'm free, nothing will shake me. Nothing. Not the wind. Not the storms. Not even an earthquake."

"Knotty, please stop!" pleaded Rooty. "You're roots aren't strong enough yet. They need more time to grow. You're making a huge mistake. Don't you remember what my momma taught us?"

"Yeah, yeah, yeah," mocked Knotty. "Your momma said we need guidelines to grow uptight. Or did she say upright? I can't remember. Any way, guidelines are for weak trees that can't stand on their own. Guidelines don't apply to strong trees like me. Besides, no matter what your Momma says, guidelines never make life better; they always make it worse."

"You're wrong, Knotty. Why would momma have called our guidelines 'lifelines' if they made life worse? For the record, she said lifelines are for the wise, not the weak. Stop acting foolish before you learn that lesson the hard way, cuz."

"I don't care what your momma said, goody two-roots. Go ahead and cling to your stupid lifelines, or whatever you choose to call them. But I'm tired of being held back."

As darkness fell, Rooty lost sight of her cousin, but she could still hear him struggling to break free. Woody, on the other hand, was in clear view, posing as usual for all to see. For the next several hours, Knotty fought for independence while Woody fought to hide his insecurity—to protect his image, to save face, and to conceal his fear of the wind.

○ ○ ○

Throughout the night the strong winds battered the town. Woody battled to resist, unwilling to let the wind get the best of him. He had a lot riding on his ability to stand firm. His success, his status, his very identity all depended upon his job performance. Getting knocked off his post and out of the spotlight would be humiliating.

Rooty, on the other hand, was still frustrated by her conversation with Knotty, so she decided to let off some oxygen. Unlike her cousin, Rooty was grateful for her lifelines. She relied on the support they provided, especially on windy days. Trusting in her lifelines gave her the freedom to relax. Knowing they kept her firmly planted allowed Rooty to engage in an elegant dance with the wind. It felt great to let down her leaves, stretch her trunk, and celebrate life for awhile.

A short time later, the wind shifted into high gear. Several times Rooty's trunk actually felt like it was going to

> **What's the big deal anyway?**

snap in two, but she knew she was built to sway in the wind, so she chose not to worry about it. Instead, she simply went along for the joyride.

In between dances, Rooty called out to see how Woody and her cousin were doing. When Knotty did not respond to her repeated calls, she thought, *He's probably just sulking.*

"I'm doing great," said Woody. "How are you, little lady?" Woody had been hiding behind his I've-got-it-all-together mask for so long, he didn't know how to take it off anymore, even when talking with his best friend.

"I'm having a blast," replied Rooty as another gust pushed her farther away from Woody.

"It sounds like it. It must be nice to have roots. Not all of us are so lucky," huffed Woody, unable to conceal his feelings.

"Are you sure you're okay, Woody? You look a little tired and sound pretty stressed out." Rooty had a knack for hearing between the lines. She could tell Woody was struggling, but she didn't expect him to admit it. Rooty never could figure out why Woody was so consumed with projecting and protecting his image. She wondered, *What's the big deal anyway?* Rooty kept an eye on her best friend as he continued to fight against the wind.

"Don't be ridiculous. Why would I be stressed out? Gusty doesn't intimidate me. Hey, Rooty, not that it matters, but how much harder do you think the wind will blow tonight? I mean, how long can Gusty keep this up anyway?" asked Woody.

When Rooty didn't respond, he yelled louder. "Rooty, can you hear me? Rooty?" Calling out was no use. As darkness fell, Gusty howled louder than a freight train, leaving Woody feeling isolated and afraid.

Gusty didn't let up all night. In addition to preventing the friends from talking, the strong winds made it impossible to sleep. At times, even Rooty's faith was tested as the wind stretched her lifelines to the limit. From where she stood, it looked like Woody was battling for his life. *I hope Knotty wised up. Without lifelines I can't imagine any tree could withstand this wind,* thought Rooty.

◯ ◯ ◯

The next morning, the donut shop owner returned to reinforce Woody's post. Based upon their past experience together, the donut man was surprised to find the sign still standing. It had been a brutal and terrifying night and Gusty was still at it. In fact, his howling kept Woody from hearing the truck pull up right beneath him. Although Woody was completely exhausted, he made his best effort not to show it—but deep down inside, he knew that he could not hang on much longer.

The shop owner knew it too. That's why he grabbed two pieces of wood, a hammer, and some nails from the truck and set out to save the sign. The first nail caught Woody completely by surprise.

"Ouch!" he screamed. "Rooty, what was that?"

Woody assumed the wind still prevented his friend from

hearing him. Several nails later, Woody realized what was happening to him. *The shop owner must be adding braces like he did the last time,* Woody thought to himself. Although the supporting braces gave Woody's aching, tired post a much-needed rest, he continued to worry about his future.

Rooty didn't spend much time worrying about her future; at least not in the traditional sense of the word. But she never lost sight of her dream: to see the Sun for the first time. Rooty preferred living in the moment, and for the moment she was having the time of her life. As the wind tossed her back and forth, she noticed the store owner dropped by to visit her friend. She wondered, *What's he doing to Woody?* Just then, another gust appeared on the scene, vaulting her forward on an amazing joyride.

Rooty loved the feeling of the wind whipping through her branches. It was exhilarating. *It feels so great to stretch my trunk. I'm so glad I'm a palm tree; otherwise, I'd be bored stiff,* she thought to herself. *Or worse yet, I'd be constantly uptight like Woody over there.*

"Whoa!" An unexpected gust caught her off guard. It slammed her sideways, nearly yanking her immature roots from the ground, but it was worth the risk. After dreaming of this moment for years, Rooty couldn't believe it was actually happening. Gusty escorted her to the perfect position, giving her the optimal angle to see past Wally, and to catch her first glimpse of the Sun. *What a moment!*

"Yes! Yes! I finally saw him! Yahoo!" exclaimed Rooty. Although she believed in the Sun and had felt his warm touch on her back many times, she had started to wonder if she would ever see him face-to-face. The buildings were just too high—before now, that is. Thanks to Gusty, the young palm tree's dream had come true. Rooty was unable to wrap her mind around what she'd just seen. The Sun looked more glorious and spectacular than she had ever imagined.

"Woo hoo!" She would never forget this moment. It was indelibly etched into her mind. In some ways, she felt different, in others the same. *Did I really just see the Sun, or is my mind just playing tricks on me?* It had all happened so quickly, so unexpectedly. But deep down inside, she knew the truth. *I definitely saw him that time. Wow, he's amazing!*

"Wally. Wally! I saw him. I saw the Sun!" Rooty wished the old building was awake. She relied on him to make sense of things. Lately, he seemed to be sleeping more and helping her sort things out less.

Ever since leaving the nursery, Rooty clung to everything her mother taught her about life. As she continued to dance with the wind, she reflected on how much her mother loved the Sun. From early on, it was obvious to Rooty that every aspect of her mother's life revolved around the Sun.

After Rooty was transplanted from the nursery to the center of the park, she relied upon Wally and Sammy the seagull to teach her about life. They did their best to pick up where her mother had left off. Day after day, they patiently answered her questions about the Sun. Both of them had spent a lot of time with him over the years.

Although Rooty had only caught a quick glimpse of the Sun, deep down inside she felt he had seen her too. Like Wally and Sammy, Rooty was grateful that she had the opportunity to see him. The Sun was incredible. He was breathtaking. So big, so powerful, and so radiant—yet his touch was so reassuring and gentle. The more she reflected on her brief encounter, the more she wondered, *Did I find the Sun or did he find me?*

One glimpse of the Sun and Rooty's quest was underway. Her entire perspective on life changed in an instant. There would be no looking back. There would be no need to look back, because she had achieved her dream. She had seen the Sun, face to face. Rooty felt different inside, changed, loved—connected to something bigger. She couldn't describe why things seemed different after such a short visit, but that didn't stop her from believing that they were.

The two most noticeable changes Rooty experienced were a burning desire to spend more time with the Sun and a newfound appreciation for the role storms play in life. She no longer was afraid of the wind. Somehow, at least on a subconscious level, she understood that the wind was actually her ticket to achieving her new dream, which was to see and talk directly to the Sun. From that day forward, Rooty stopped seeing the high winds and storms as a threat to her safety. Instead, she began viewing them as a means to an end; the secret to growing stronger roots.

○ ○ ○

Rooty was having the best day of her life. Woody looked like he was having his worst. He flinched and stiffened up every time he heard the wind approaching. Even though her roots were aching, Rooty yearned to catch another glimpse of the Sun. So when the next gust of wind whipped across the park, she cupped her branches, hoping to extend her joyride.

Although she didn't see the Sun, her strategy worked. "Wahoo!" she blurted out, as she lurched forward. A sharp pain surged through her roots, followed by a strange tingling sensation. Fortunately, both quickly went away. If it weren't for her lifelines, she'd most certainly have fallen flat on her face. Despite the risk, she was getting ready to take another joyride when the sight of Woody struggling to keep his balance drew her attention. *I can't enjoy myself while Woody is over there holding on for dear life,* she thought to herself.

Rooty didn't know how to help her friend, but she definitely knew what his problem was. Woody's happiness revolved around his job. If his position was threatened, he was miserable. He had never told Rooty, but it was pretty obvious; almost every conversation revolved around his ability to project an image. *All work and no play has certainly made Woody a pretty boring sign,* thought Rooty. *But I love watching out for him anyway.*

"Woody, are you okay?" asked Rooty.

"Never been better."

"Really? What was the shop owner doing to you?" she inquired.

"I think he's planning to put some smaller signs beneath me. You know, he probably wants to promote me since I'm doing such a great job."

Woody knew this wasn't the case, but he was too embarrassed to admit the truth—he was having trouble standing on his own. Sometimes, Woody wished he could just let his guard down. He wished that he could stop projecting an image for awhile, but it was a difficult habit to break. After spending years pretending to have it all together, Woody didn't know how to take his mask off, even with his best friend.

"Funny, they don't look like signs. There's no writing on them. Besides—"

"Rooty, enough about me," Woody interrupted, hoping to deflect the attention away from his shortcomings. "What have you been doing this morning? Anything productive?"

"If you call achieving your lifelong dream productive, then yes. I'm having a fantastic morning. I found the Sun! Can you believe it? I finally saw him. I thought this day might never come. My mother was right; he's incredible."

Sometimes, I wonder if she'll ever grow up, Woody thought to himself. He did his best to be positive, but her carefree lifestyle really annoyed him at times. "That's what all the fuss was about? Finding the Sun? What's the big deal anyway? It's not like you weren't sure he was out there. I haven't seen him for years, but you don't see me worrying about it, do you? Besides, you act like you're the first one ever to find him," replied Woody.

"You might not be worried about seeing the Sun, but you sure look worried about keeping your job," retorted Rooty. The instant the words left her mouth, she regretted saying them. She was about to apologize when Woody fired back.

"Well, excuse me, missy. Sorry if I look worried about doing my job. The shop owner is counting on me, you know. Oh, I'm sorry. You wouldn't know what that's like, now would you? You

Can you believe it?

haven't worked a day in your life, and you probably never will."

Rooty's feelings were hurt. She didn't know what to say, but she knew what she *wasn't* going to say: I'm sorry. She wrestled with her thoughts. Woody had finally crossed the line. Fortunately for him, her momma's voice was echoing in the back of her mind, keeping her at bay. *Rooty, when others bark at you, don't bark back. It will only splinter your friendships.* She knew her mother was right. That didn't make it any easier, though. She wondered, *Would he ever change? Would he ever see the truth about life? Would he ever stop seeking the spotlight?*

Woody, satisfied that he had made his point, turned his attention back to resisting the wind. Despite the additional supporting braces, he knew he was in for a long day.

○ ○ ○

Later that afternoon, after reflecting on her conversation with Woody, Rooty had a change of heart. She decided to apologize to her friend, even though the whole thing was his fault. Before she had time to change her mind, Rooty said, "Woody, I'm sorry about what I said." Unfortunately, Gusty appeared out of nowhere and carried her words away before they reached their intended destination.

Meanwhile, Woody was totally focused on his own situation. He desperately wished that the storm would blow over and the wind would disappear. Gusty, as if he overheard Woody's earlier claim about not being intimidated by the wind, revved up for another round. After recharging his blower, Gusty launched a full-out frontal attack. In a series of short bursts, one after the other, he proved to be too much for the sign. First, Woody's extra support braces gave way. Then, just seconds later, an updraft plucked his post right out of the ground like an undesirable weed.

A final gust finished the job by slamming Woody flat on his back. The damage was more mental than physical. Nothing was broken. He was conscious. And he was still connected to his post, but his ego was severely bruised. *Here we go again. My image is ruined. How am I ever going to explain this away this time?* he asked himself.

The last time Woody got knocked off his post was several years back. Even though he'd been through this before, it never got any easier. As a matter of fact, it seemed harder now that he was a bigger sign. From his perspective, the fact that he was more visible in town created increased pressure to perform.

As he lay there frustrated and embarrassed, doubt overtook him. *The store owner will help get me back on my feet, won't he? I mean, without me, how can he draw attention to the shop? He needs me, right? What if he doesn't?* His mind raced. Images of junk being piled on top of him at the junkyard swirled in his head. *What if he's tired of picking me up? What would happen to me if I didn't have this job? Could I find another? What would come of me then?* Anxiety and fear consumed him. He couldn't think about anything else. He began to sob.

Rooty witnessed the entire thing. It was painful to watch. Now, she could hear him weeping, so she called out to him. "Don't worry, Woody. You're going to be okay. In fact, you'll be better than okay. This will make you stronger," Rooty assured her friend.

"Make me stronger? What in the world are you talking about?" Woody sniped back.

"My momma taught Knotty and me to embrace the wind, not to fight it. She told us that the wind is our friend, because the wind helps our roots grow stronger," responded Rooty. "And she said we need strong roots if we're going to grow closer to the Sun."

"That's the stupidest—" Gusty kicked up a sandstorm, choking off the rest of Woody's comment.

What in the world are you talking about?

The sandstorm didn't affect Rooty, so she continued her thought. "Here's what Momma used to tell Knotty and me. 'There will be days when the wind will make it difficult to stand. On those days remember to turn *two* into *four*. Stop asking, "Why is this happening *to* me?" and start asking, "Why is this happening *for* me?"'"

"Rooty, that's the stupidest thing you've ever said! First of all, I don't have roots like you. So, the wind doesn't make me stronger, it only makes it harder for me to do my job. Secondly, take a good look at me. I'm lying flat on my back here. Now you're going to try and convince me that, somehow, this is happening *for* me and not *to* me? Turn two into four, how ridiculous," mumbled Woody to himself before lashing out one last time. "Where did your momma come up with that one? Oh, let me guess. The Sun probably told her."

"It is not ridiculous. It's true. Knotty, go ahead and tell him that it's true. Tell him. Knotty?"

Rooty had been so focused on straightening out Woody that she hadn't noticed her cousin was down for the count too. He was lying motionless, helplessly on the ground right next to his lifelines. Apparently he had finally shrugged free.

"Oh no! Knotty, can you hear me? Knotty, say something!" *How long has he been down? Is anyone going to help him?*

Rooty called out to her cousin throughout the night. Eventually she cried herself to sleep. Woody was past the crying stage, so he lay awake worrying about his future.

○ ○ ○

The next morning, the shop owner stood over the sign. His hands rested on his hips, while his frown telegraphed his frustration. "This isn't good," he said to his wife. "It's not like the old days when I could just lift him up by myself and put him back on his post. He's gotten too big for me to do that now."

"So, what do you propose?" asked his wife as she placed her hand on his arm, trying to comfort him somehow.

"I don't know. With more storms heading our way, I'm not sure propping him back up would be a wise investment. He's gotten so top heavy that the wind is just having its way with him," he sighed.

The words burned the sign's ears. "Top heavy? Look who's talking. You might want to lay off the donuts, big guy," retorted Woody. Fortunately, the shop owner didn't understand sign language or Woody would have sealed his fate.

Woody's greatest fear was quickly becoming reality. Even Rooty, who was the poster child for optimism, was shaken to the core by the shop owner's comments. This was not turning out to be a very good morning. Woody and Knotty were both down, and Knotty hadn't moved or responded to her calls. *Turning two into four is easier said than done,* she thought to herself.

I sure wish Momma were here to pray for Knotty and Woody. Rooty's mother said the best prayers. They always left Rooty feeling hopeful about the future. The young tree closed her eyes. *I wonder if I could pray on my own? Momma always said that anybody could do it once they grew close enough to the Sun. I wonder if I'm close enough yet? How tall do I need to be anyway?*

Before Rooty could muster the strength to try talking directly to the Sun, she was interrupted by a loud, screeching noise. When Rooty opened her eyes, she saw the tree doctor pulling his long flatbed truck up next to Knotty.

"Woody, look!" shouted Rooty enthusiastically. "The tree doctor has come to check on Knotty. He knows trees better than anyone. At least that's what Momma used to say. Anyway, he definitely knows Knotty, because he's the one who raised us when we were just saplings."

"That's just great," replied Woody, sarcastically. "However, need I remind you that unless he knows sign language, it won't do me any good."

Rooty felt sorry for her friend. She could hear the fear and anxiety in Woody's voice, and she could tell that he was really struggling. So she thought to herself, *After the tree doctor cures Knotty, I'll try asking the Sun to send help for Woody too.*

The tree doctor pulled a snakelike metal object off the truck and wrapped it around Knotty's trunk. Rooty watched as he connected the other end to a long, rusty arm protruding from the top of the truck and flipped the switch. The whirring sound coming from the crane hurt Rooty's ears, but she quickly got over it when Knotty began to move.

"Knotty, you're awake. How do you feel?" asked Rooty. Knotty didn't respond. *Maybe he can't hear me over all that noise.* "Knotty, it's the tree doctor. He's come to save you," she shouted. "Hang in there, cuz. Everything is going to be okay. I just know it."

○ ○ ○

Later that same day, the dark storm clouds approached slowly as the store owner stood over Woody once again. This time, several other people joined him, including the tree doctor. Woody listened as the shop owner introduced the people to each other.

"Everyone, meet everyone. That cheerful looking character over there is Trey. He owns the nursery down the road. As you can see from the sweat on his brow, he's already been working hard this morning." Trey nodded to the others. "This sharp young lady to my left is Ann. She's the best architect in the whole state, and Carl here is a gifted carpenter."

Ann and Carl both blushed at the unsolicited compliments as the shop owner continued. "Carl is the one who helped Eddie make this old sign. Eddie owns both the lumberyard and the junkyard outside of town. That way he's involved, whether we're building something or tearing it down. Ain't that right, Eddie? And you all know my oldest son, Danny."

Rooty looked on as each of them shook hands and said hello to one another. She noticed that Danny greeted the others differently than the rest. Instead of shaking their hands, he hugged each of them. Then he gently reached out and touched their faces. Rooty had seen him do this to the children in the park many times, but she didn't understand why he was doing it now. *Why is he tickling everyone? This is no time to be fooling around,* she thought to herself. *Can't he see that Woody and Knotty are in trouble?*

"I've called all of you here this morning to seek your input. We desperately need your advice. My wife and I just don't know what to do with this old sign anymore. We'd like to salvage him, but we can't afford to keep standing him back up. Now with the added expense of hauling that tree off, well…" The shop owner's voice trailed off as the group loomed over Woody.

Woody could feel their presence, but nobody was saying anything. "Rooty. Rooty! What are they doing? Can you see what they're doing?" Woody was no longer pretending to be strong. His words dripped with desperation.

"They're just standing there. They are not doing anything," she replied.

"Where is Knotty?" he asked.

"He's lying down on the back of the tree doctor's truck.

I guess he's sleeping. I've been trying to talk to him, but he's not responding."

"Rooty, he's not sleeping. Didn't you hear what the shop owner just said? They're hauling him off…oh no! They're going to take both of us to the junkyard! My parents warned me that this day would come."

Woody was an emotional wreck. He was falling apart. Before Rooty could console him, it began raining in sheets. The shop owner and the others covered their heads and ran for shelter. By the time the last one of them had ducked into the donut shop, Woody's imagination had already gotten the best of him.

I'm a goner. Gusty's destroyed my future. I hate him! Woody took a deep breath, trying to gather his composure, but it was no use. *The shop owner is definitely going to replace me. Why else would he bring all those people here?* Woody's pity party shifted into full gear. He began to sob uncontrollably as his tears mixed with the rain.

Rooty's tiny ears soaked up Woody's words while her thirsty roots vacuumed up a much needed drink. "*They're going to take both of us to the junkyard. Our lives are over.*" Although the water was refreshing and went up smoothly, Woody's words were hard to swallow. As she replayed them in her mind, they sapped her spirit. Rooty felt sad and ached all over. She couldn't think straight. She didn't know where to turn, what to do, or whom to talk to. Eventually she became so distraught that her earlier thoughts of trying to talk with the Sun washed away with the rain.

The young palm tree had never been this sad before. She felt like crying, but she couldn't find the strength to release a single tear. Rooty couldn't imagine a day ever getting worse than this one had been.

◯ ◯ ◯

When the rain finally stopped, the people emerged from the donut shop, hopped into their cars, and drove off. The only people who remained were the shop owner, the tree doctor, and Danny. Woody could hear them approaching.

"Rooty, who's that coming toward me?"

"It's just the shop owner and Danny." She hated to lie, but Woody was already disturbed enough.

As the three men stood over Woody, Danny whispered something into his father's ear. His father immediately turned and headed back towards the shop. Then Danny whispered something to the tree doctor, who turned around to look at Knotty lying on the truck. "You know, that just might work," replied Trey.

Nobody, including Rooty, who was leavesdropping on their conversation, heard what Danny had whispered to either man. However, Rooty heard what Danny said next, loud and clear. Unfortunately, Woody heard it too.

"It's like the *Good Book* says, 'At least there is hope for a tree: If it is cut down, it will sprout again, and its new shoots will not fail. Its roots may grow old in the ground and its stump die in the soil, yet at the scent of water, it will bud and put forth shoots like a plant.'"

Rooty didn't fully understand what Danny had recited, but the passion in his voice renewed her sense of hope. Deep down inside, she believed that Woody and Knotty would recover from their injuries.

Do you think anyone will remember me?

"Rooty, even if they get me back on my post, who's to say another storm won't come along and knock me flat on my back, again. It's inevitable that at some point, they will just toss me aside. Do you think anyone will remember me? Do you think they will talk about me after I'm gone?"

Rooty had never heard Woody talk this way before. His normal air of self-confidence was noticeably absent. She didn't know how to respond, so she said, "Why don't you ask Wally? He's much wiser than I am. He's been around longer and has more experience. That's why I always seek his advice when life doesn't make sense."

Woody heeded his friend's advice and called over to Wally.

"Rooty, can you see if his eyes are closed? He's not answering me." Woody had never shown much patience with the old building.

Unfortunately for Woody, Wally was fast asleep. Rooty wished she could offer Woody sound advice. She tried to remember some of the life lessons her mother had taught her about the Sun, but she was too distracted. She still couldn't figure Danny out. *What's his secret? What did Danny whisper to the shop owner? Why did he run off?*

A few seconds later, Rooty knew one thing for certain. Whatever Danny had whispered to his father couldn't have been good.

ɔ ɔ ɔ

The door to the donut shop swung open and the shop owner bolted out. He headed straight for Woody. A long, orange extension cord trailed behind him. The possessed look
on his face frightened Rooty. In his left hand he clutched
an object that looked like the toy guns Rooty had seen the
boys playing with in the park. In his right hand, Rooty
could see a shiny circular object. As he raced toward Danny
and Trey, he was trying to connect the two objects.

"Is that the biggest auger you have?" asked the tree doctor.

"Don't worry, doctor," replied the shop owner. "It might
take a little longer to finish the job, but once I drill enough
baseball-size holes in him, standing upright will be the least
of his problems. This old sign won't be tangling with the
wind anymore after today. Mark my words on that; those
days are behind us. Right, Danny?"

Danny nodded.

Meanwhile, the moment Rooty heard the word drill, a
chill ran down her trunk. Instantly, she feared the worst.
Her mother had warned her about power tools. She told
her they were a tree's worst enemy—even worse than a
woodpecker.

"Wally, did you hear that?" asked Rooty, trying to mask
the concern in her voice so as not to disturb Woody. "What
should we do? We have to stop him before it's too late."
*Man, Wally. How can you sleep through all this? What's up
with you lately?*

Rooty took one more look at the power drill and, feeling she had no other choice, screamed for Woody to pro-

tect himself. "Watch out, Woody, he's heading straight for you!"

Prior to that moment, Woody never had any reason to fear the shop owner. But the panic in Rooty's voice convinced him that he had good reason to now. He braced himself for the worst as he desperately tried to stand up. He wanted to prove that he was still the best sign for the job, but it was too late. The shop owner already stood squarely on top of him, making it extremely difficult to breathe.

For the next few minutes, all Rooty could hear was the high-pitched screeching of the metal piercing through Woody's tough veneer. The shop owner had gone mad. He was punching one hole after another into Woody. Rooty couldn't bear to watch. Nor could she stand listening to the sound of the auger going in and out of Woody, over and over again. It was horrific. Rooty pulled her branches over her head, but it didn't help. *I've got to do something. I can't just stand by and watch them destroy Woody,* she thought to herself.

Not knowing what else to do, Rooty cried out to the Sun, "You have to stop him. You have to save Woody. Please!" She hoped he would hear her because from her vantage point, barring a miracle, Woody wouldn't survive this attack.

○ ○ ○

As darkness fell, Rooty's trunk ached and she felt empty inside; rotten and lifeless. She was completely drained from crying all day. She had no more tears to offer. Shortly after the shop owner's attack ended, the tree doctor drove off with Knotty. Woody hadn't moved or responded to Rooty's calls since the men left. Worse yet, the Sun had ignored her cry for help. Several more times, she called out to him through the thick dark clouds, but he was nowhere to be found. *How could you abandon Woody, Knotty, and me when we needed you most? My momma said you would always be there for me. I guess Momma was wrong.*

Rooty couldn't imagine how she could ever forget this day or erase the picture of Woody being attacked from her memory. While she was lost in thought, Gusty snuck up behind her and whipped her violently forward. This time, she was in no mood for an adventure. She stiffened her trunk in order to deny him the satisfaction of swaying her. She had no intention of celebrating her flexibility or playing along this time. *The last thing I want to do is encourage Gusty after what he's done to Woody.*

The cool damp air added to Rooty's blue mood as she reflected on the events from the past two days. *How could the best day of my life be followed by my worst? It doesn't make any sense.* Rooty had never lost anyone she loved before now. Admittedly, it was hard to say goodbye to her mother and father when she had left the nursery, but this was different. Her mother and father were still alive. At least that's what Sammy the seagull told her the last time she asked him to check in on them. Having watched the shop owner turn on Woody, she now wondered, *Can I trust Sammy to tell me the truth? Can anyone trust anyone, anymore?*

The fact that the Sun hadn't immediately responded

Can anyone trust
anyone, anymore?

to Rooty's plea for help disturbed her deeply. At one point, later in the day, she even began questioning all the life lessons her mother, Wally, and Sammy had taught her. Her eyelids grew heavy as she questioned, *Who can I believe anymore?*

As Rooty drifted off to sleep, she dreamt of her childhood days back in the nursery. She listened to her mother's gentle voice telling one of her amazing stories. She was as happy as could be, laughing along with Knotty and the other saplings. Mainly, though, she was studying her mother's every move. The young tree admired her mother. She hoped to grow up to be just like her one day.

Rooty slept on and off for almost two days. At times she had difficulty separating her dreams from reality. When she finally woke up, the Sun had broken through the clouds and was gently caressing her back. If Rooty hadn't been rooted in place, she would have thrown herself on the ground or run away from the Sun, like a child having a tantrum. After what had happened to Knotty and Woody, she wasn't sure she ever wanted to see him again.

The strong winds died down. All that remained was the typical coastal breeze. Rooty noticed the dark, gloomy clouds had been replaced with bright, fluffy white ones. At first, she thought she was still dreaming, like she was floating amidst the clouds. The inside of her head felt fuzzy and her thinking was unclear. One of her mother's favorite sayings rattled around in her head. "Rooty, things aren't always as they appear. Just keep looking up, looking inside, and looking out for others."

A horn honked on the street below, startling Rooty. The sudden noise yanked her out of her dreamlike state and vaulted her back into the present moment. She glanced quickly to the right and then to the left. Reality came sweeping back in. Knotty was gone and Woody was still lying flat on his back.

○ ○ ○

The red pickup truck sputtered down Main Street and pulled up next to where Woody was lying. After it came to a complete stop, both doors swung open. As the two men emerged from the truck, Rooty focused on the driver. She didn't recognize him. The passenger, on the other hand, she would never forget—nor would she ever forgive the shop owner, after what he had done to her best friend. *Now what's he up to?*

Rooty wanted to take a closer look, so she cupped her branches and used the ocean breeze to lean in their direction. The driver was an odd-looking character, different from the shop owner in almost every way. He was quite a sight to behold. Not only was he younger and smaller than the donut man, he was more colorful too. He had an energetic spirit and a bright outfit to match. He wore a multi-colored T-shirt, a purple brimless hat, and had silver hoops dangling from his ears. His hat was tilted awkwardly to the right side of his head. *He's quite a character,* thought Rooty, *and he's fun to watch. What's that on his arm?*

The wind died down temporarily, returning Rooty to her upright position. She waited, branches cupped, for another breeze to take her in for a closer look. *It's a heart. He's got a heart painted on his forearm. I think I'm going to like him.* Rooty watched as the younger man walked slowly

around the pickup truck and over toward Woody. The way
he walked was consistent with his outfit. There was a joyful spring to his step. The tops of his bare feet were golden
brown.

All this made the colorful young man all the more fun
to watch. The two men stood looking at Woody for a moment before the younger man sauntered over to the bed of
the pickup truck, reached in, and pulled out a shovel. Rooty
had seen plenty of shovels in her day and been warned by
her mother about the danger they posed to her roots.

Again, Rooty could practically hear her mother's voice
saying, "Rooty, protecting your roots is vital to your sur-
vival out there in the real world. Once your roots are established, do whatever you can to avoid contact with shovels.
A run in with a shovel could be fatal."

"Here you go, old man. Have at it," he said, as he handed the shovel to the shop owner.

Have at it? Oh no, he's going to attack Woody again.
"Woody, watch out. He's got a shovel. Protect your roots, if
you've got any…" Rooty's voice trailed off as she watched
the shop owner smile and shake his head from side to side.
*How dare he smile at a time like this?! What's come over him?
I thought he loved Woody.*

As the shop owner started digging, the younger man
strolled over to investigate a long wooden object lying on
the ground next to Woody. *That's weird,* thought Rooty. *I
don't remember seeing that before. How did it get there? What's
it for? I wonder how long I've been asleep.* As she watched the
young man take a closer look she thought, *It looks a little*

bit like a tree, but it can't be a tree, because it doesn't have any leaves.

Having surveyed the scene the colorful young man stretched out on the ground, covered his face with his hat, and took a nap. For the next two hours, he slept while the shop owner dug a large hole. It looked like it might be a while before Rooty figured out what the two men were up to. In the meantime, despite her attempt to remain hopeful a terrible thought crossed her mind. *Could he be digging a grave for Woody?*

The thought made her stomach ache. Rooty tried to distract herself by watching a young boy in the park. He tossed oyster crackers in the air and laughed uncontrollably as the seagulls swarmed above his head, competing for the free grub. The wind carried the boy's laughter across the park to where Rooty was standing. Although she couldn't explain it, she noticed that somehow the boy's laughter boosted her spirits. She was glad he was there. *The last thing I need is to be alone with my thoughts right now.*

◯ ◯ ◯

Rooty, remember: Things aren't always as they appear. The scene too often conceals the truth. Just keep looking up, looking inside, and looking out for others. Her mother's words rose from the deep recesses of her mind, or at least she assumed they were her mother's words. Lately, Rooty was really struggling to clear her mind. Separating the voices in her head from reality was nearly impossible. Regardless of the source, she couldn't get this riddle out of her head, and it was about to drive her crazy.

As she watched the people walking in an out of Wally's front door, Rooty decided to ask the old building if he knew what the riddle meant.

"Wally, are you awake?" she asked.

"Hello, little lady," responded Wally in a raspy but kind voice. "How are you doing this glorious morning?"

Glorious? Which direction have you been looking in? Rooty knew the old building's hearing and eyesight were deteriorating, *But how could he miss this?* she thought to herself. *Wally hasn't said a word about what's happened to Woody and Knotty. That's not like him.*

"Actually, given everything that's happened, I'm pretty upset," she replied.

"Oh, I'm sorry to hear that, Rooty. Would you like to talk about it?" asked Wally, as he did his best to suppress a yawn.

The old building didn't want Rooty to get the wrong impression. *The last thing I want is for Rooty to think I don't care, because nothing could be further from the truth.* Wally loved the little tree like a daughter, and he knew the events over the past two days must have really shaken her.

Rooty was perplexed. *He acts like my being upset is a surprise. How did he expect me to feel?* Rooty thought about asking Wally why he wasn't more upset. Given everything that had happened, he sure seemed oblivious to the situation. After thinking about it for a minute, she thought, *Maybe talking about it makes him too sad. Yeah, that's probably it. I'll just let him deal with the loss of Woody and Knotty in his own way.*

Which direction have you been looking in?

Rather than pressing the issue, Rooty shared the riddle with Wally instead. She hoped the wise old building could translate the life lesson echoing in her head. Deep down inside, the young tree sensed that the riddle contained the secret to her finding happiness again, even in the middle of this storm.

"I sure wish I could meet your mother someday, Rooty. I like the way she thinks."

"Does that mean you solved the riddle?"

"Well, not exactly. I've never heard it phrased quite this way before, but I think I get the gist of it. Basically, she's saying, 'Don't believe everything you see, look beyond your current circumstances, and be a blessing to others.'"

The first two pieces of advice sounded familiar, the third was new, so Rooty asked, "What do you mean 'be a blessing to others'?"

"Rooty, I'm sure your mother must have taught you the Golden Rule, right?"

"Sure. Momma encouraged Knotty and me to memorize it," replied Rooty before reciting it with ease. "Do to others what you would have them do to you."

Wally could tell Rooty still didn't see the connection. "Rooty, being a blessing to others means placing their needs ahead of your own. When we're busy doing something for someone else we spend less time worrying about our own situation. Are you tracking with me, little lady?"

The young palm tree's expression told Wally he needed to try yet again. "Rooty, it's in giving to others that we receive."

Now Rooty was really confused. "Giving what and getting what?" she asked.

"Rooty, you'll just have to experience it for yourself to understand it. Trust me, little lady, your mother is a wise tree. Something tells me that it won't be long before you grow up to be just like her. So sway along now, Rooty. Go make your momma proud by serving others. Give and you will receive, and in no time you'll be feeling better than ever inside. I promise."

Giving what and getting what?

○ ○ ○

Although Rooty didn't totally understand the riddle, feeling better sounded like a great idea. So the hopeful young tree decided to give this serving-others thing a whirl. She looked up at the blue sky, straightened her trunk, and released a burst of oxygen. As she did, she recalled her mother commenting on how people depended upon trees to clean the air so they could breathe. *I'm not sure how all that stuff works, but maybe if I breathe more, it will serve more people.*

Rooty spent the next few minutes huffing and puffing. She stopped when she began feeling dizzy to focus on whatever was tickling her trunk. Looking down, she realized it was the tiny feet of the three gecko kids. She hadn't seen them since Gusty first appeared on the scene. They appeared to be fighting as they chased each other in circles around her trunk. In an effort to break up the squabble, Rooty twisted her trunk and cupped her branches. The wind jolted her forward, instantly attracting the gecko kids' attention.

Despite the way it appeared, the gecko kids were not fighting. They were playing follow the leader. Rooty figured this out the moment she leaned forward and heard the leader say, "Told you this was the coolest tree in the park. Now it's your turn to lead."

Knowing they appreciated her put a smile on Rooty's face. She seized the opportunity to serve the gecko kids, twisting the opposite way to offer the new leader a more challenging course.

Meanwhile, Rooty noticed a squadron of pelicans gliding overhead. She greeted them with a wave of her branches and a friendly smile. "Your formation sure looks great this morning, guys."

"And you appear to be getting closer to the Sun every day, missy," replied the pelican with the golden head. "If you get any taller, we'll have to fly around you instead of over you," he chuckled. "Have a great day."

Gosh, this serving others thing really seems to work, she thought to herself. *I wonder if it's always this easy to do.* Rooty was already beginning to experience the benefits of serving others. *Wally was right. I'm starting to feel better inside already. I bet if...*

Before Rooty could finish her thought, the odd-looking young man in the purple hat arose from his slumber. After stretching for a moment, he stood up and walked over to the truck. He let down the flap on the back and started pulling out a large wooden box. It must have been really heavy, because he asked the shop owner to help him pick it up. Working together, they carried it around the truck and set it down next to Woody. The older man walked toward the donut shop and the younger man ducked behind the truck, leaving Rooty all alone in the park.

She watched for awhile, but neither of them reappeared, so she looked in the direction of the familiar squawking sound just in time to see Sammy the seagull coasting along like a kite. Rooty called out to him, "Sammy, can you come over here please?"

With a slight tilt of his wings, Sammy caught an updraft and glided effortlessly over to the center of the park to visit his favorite tree. "Hey, Rooty, how have you been?" Sammy hovered gracefully above her as he waited for a response.

"I'm doing much better. Thanks for asking. Hey, can you do me a favor?" she asked.

"Sure. How can I be of service to you this morning, young lady?" replied Sammy.

His comment struck a chord, causing her to hesitate for a moment. *He's offering to serve me. I wonder if he learned that from my momma.* "Sammy, can you please fly over there and see what that young man behind the red pickup truck is doing?" she asked in a friendly but concerned tone.

Prior to that moment, Sammy, who had spent the past couple of days raiding the dumpsters on the mainland, hadn't noticed that Woody was lying flat on his back. "Hey, what happened to Woody?" asked Sammy

"What hasn't? First Gusty knocked him down. Then the store owner attacked him. Now I can't figure out what's going on. That's why I need your help."

"You got it. I'll be back in a flash."

The seagull swooped in and circled the truck several times, like a fighter pilot on a mission. Then as promised, he zipped back to give Rooty his report.

"I'm not sure what he's doing, but it looks like a gravesite over there. They've dug a big hole. Hope that helps, gotta fly. The kids on the beach have another box of crackers. See you later, Rooty."

"A gravesite?" she muttered. "Sammy, wait!" But it was too late. Sammy had already joined the squawking aerial ballet.

Rooty marveled at the way the seagulls embraced the wind and put it to work for them. Sammy had been the one who taught her how to cup her branches to catch an updraft. She watched as he effortlessly tilted his wings and hung suspended in midair. Then, at just the right moment, he swooped down and snatched a cracker right out of the boy's hand.

○ ○ ○

Shortly thereafter, the young man finally emerged from behind the truck. Rooty didn't recognize him at first because he had changed outfits. He now had on a one-piece white coverall. A red bandana replaced his purple hat and a pair of clear goggles covered his eyes.

If he hadn't walked around to the driver's side of the truck, reached through the window and honked the horn, Rooty would have mistaken him for one of the doctors from the hospital. After blasting the horn he turned to face the donut shop and started waving his hands, back and forth, above his head. *He sure is a strange bird,* thought Rooty.

She watched as the donut man popped his head out of the shop and waved before disappearing again. Then he bolted out the door dragging a long orange extension cord behind him. He brought the end of the orange cord down to the younger man. The other end still appeared to be inside the shop. The young man connected the cord to some kind of power tool and revved its motor. The sound cut through the morning air, startling Rooty. Apparently it caught the donut man off guard too, because Rooty saw him flinch slightly before taking a few steps backward.

For the next few hours the young man in the white jumpsuit attacked Woody using a variety of different power tools. Each tool made quite a racket. Some even threw dust high into the air. Throughout the entire assault Woody just lay there lifeless.

Even though Rooty didn't want to watch, she found herself unable to look away. She was in shock. Yet, somehow through it all, despite all the noise and the dust a little voice inside of her kept saying, *Never lose hope. Never stop believing.*

The longer the day went on, the harder it was to maintain hope. Eventually Rooty's mindset shifted completely the other way. *Maybe what Momma told me about turning two into four was ridiculous.* She reflected back to what Sammy had said. "*It sure looks like a gravesite over there.*"

She called out to Wally only to find him fast asleep, again. As nighttime approached, the Sun dipped beyond the horizon. Rooty braced herself for another long, lonely night.

∘ ○ ◡

Carl, the carpenter, was sitting in his truck next to Woody as the Sun ushered in a new day. The shop owner and the colorful younger man had just walked out of the shop to meet him. A short while later, Trey and Eddie pulled up in the long flatbed truck; the one they used to haul Knotty off. After the men greeted each other briefly they got right to work. The tree doctor got out the long, metal snake and tied it around the long tree-like object still lying on the ground next to Woody. Then he returned to his truck and hit the switch. The straighter and tighter the metal snake got, the louder the machine whined.

This time, instead of looking away, Rooty watched closely. She studied their every move, but she had no idea what they were up to. With the other men helping to guide the long object, the machine on the truck raised it upright. Once it was high enough off the ground, they positioned it so that one end was directly over the hole that the shop owner had dug next to Woody.

The shop owner still had that smile plastered to his face. *I wish he'd come close enough so I could slap it off with one of my branches. What kind of person smiles at a funeral?* thought Rooty as the gravity of the situation sank in.

When they placed the end into the hole and raised the other end upright, hope surfaced out of nowhere. Rooty had a sudden change of heart. *It still looks like a tree to me, but it can't be. It has no roots and no branches. Hey, maybe it's a new post for Woody. Maybe today is the day they will raise him back into position.*

While the shop owner and the younger man held the

pole in place, another man, who Rooty had never seen before, pulled up in a green pickup truck and backed it up next to the men. As soon as he stopped, the men with the shovels hopped up onto the back of the truck and began shoveling dark soil into the hole. When they were finished, the tree doctor jumped up and down in a circle all around the tree. *That's a funny-looking dance,* thought Rooty.

What she didn't realize at the time was that Trey was just packing down the soil. "Okay, guys, now lay that grass over the top to keep the good soil from washing away the next time it rains."

After the pole was securely anchored, the four men approached Woody. Each one grabbed one of his corners. "Now, on the count of three, let's stand him up," said Carl. Rooty couldn't believe her ears. Nor could she believe how different Woody looked. His face was much plainer and cleaner. In fact, it was hard to tell if it was really her best friend or not. *What have they done to him?* she wondered.

The tree doctor looped the metal snake through two of the holes that the shop owner had punched into Woody. Once the snake was securely fastened, Trey flipped the switch. The motor whined louder than before, but still managed to lift the sign up off the ground. Woody was suspended in mid-air, like a yo-yo, gently swinging from side to side.

After the top of the sign was in line with the top of the pole, Carl said, "Hold it right there while I get my ladder in place."

Rooty watched as Carl quickly climbed up the so called ladder and drove some long metal spikes through Woody and into his new post. The pounding sound echoed off of Wally's brick wall and ricocheted back to where Rooty was standing.

"Ouch. Ouch! That stings. Rooty, what are they doing to me?" asked Woody.

"Woody, you're alive! Oh my gosh, you're alive!"

"Of course I'm alive, Rooty. What's wrong with you? You're not making sense. Why wouldn't I be alive?"

Rooty was dumfounded. If she hadn't been so happy to see him, she would have barked back at him. Instead, she focused on trying to figure out what had really happened. "Woody, you haven't moved or spoken since the shop owner attacked you. So I thought you were—"

"He wasn't attacking me. Rooty, sometimes you're so dramatic. He was giving me a makeover. I'm going to be a whole new sign. They told me I would look and feel better than ever. Then they warned me not to move until they were finished. They said I needed to keep my face perfectly still. I heard you calling, but I couldn't risk ruining my makeover. So how do I look?"

You may have a whole new look, but you're outlook on life is still completely self-centered, she thought to herself. It hadn't taken long for Woody to get on her roots again. She would have thought that after all he'd been through, he might have changed at least a little. *After letting me worry half to death for the past two days, now you expect me to be your mirror. Think again!*

Rooty took several deep breaths, hoping the carbon dioxide would help her regain her composure. Meanwhile, she wondered, *Does he realize he's full of holes? Should I tell him the truth about how he looks?* As irritated as she was with him, she decided not to risk hurting his feelings. Finally, after calming down, she replied, "You look really…umm… different. How do you feel?"

"I feel different—lighter and more refreshed. But I'm really, really thirsty for some reason." Woody paused for a moment, pondering something. "Hmmm, that's weird. Normally, after all that rain, I would feel waterlogged, not thirsty. Oh well, I guess the makeover must have dried me out a bit."

While Woody was going on-and-on about his make-over, Rooty got an idea. *Instead of allowing him to upset me, maybe I should try serving him the way Wally taught me to. I wonder if that would make both of us feel better.* She decided there was only one way to find out. She would try it. *The next time the pelicans fly over, I'll ask my yellow-headed friend to serve Woody a cool drink of water.*

As the sun dipped behind Wally, the blind teacher made his way from the hospital across the park and over toward where the men were standing.

"Sure, now you show up, brother," said the colorful young man. "Now that all the heavy lifting is over. I guess your getting too old for this now that you've hit the big thirty." This last comment brought a big smile to his older brother's face.

"I invited you to spend the day up at the hospital, but you teenagers never listen," replied the blind teacher. The men burst out laughing. Once they had settled back down, Danny motioned for Artie to come closer. Rooty strained to hear what he said next.

"Seriously, Artie, we could really use your ⟩
Those kids need a ray of sunshine like you to ⟩
day. Some of them don't have many days lef⟩
The invitation's always open, little brother."

The humor had provided a nice ending to a hard day's work. "Great work, guys. I owe you one. Let's call it a day. I don't know about the rest of you, but my back is killing me," said the shop owner.

The colorful young man, who Rooty now realized was named Artie, agreed. "Yeah, I am bushed too. However, I'm sure it's nothing that a few donuts can't fix. Got any extras for the ride home?" he added with a smile.

Rooty watched as the men went their separate ways.

Even though she couldn't see him, Rooty could always tell when the Sun was getting ready to dip below the horizon because she watched the shadows. The lower the Sun went, the longer the shadows got. When the ones cast by Wally and the other buildings reached the park bench in front of her, Rooty knew the day was just about over. A few minutes later, Rooty found herself standing alone in the dark with her thoughts. *I remember how upset I got with the Sun the day the shop owner attacked Woody. I couldn't believe he had ignored my cry for help.*

Was he listening the whole time? He certainly seems to have saved Woody from the grave. Hmmm…maybe I was a little hasty in the way I judged him, she thought to herself as she drifted off to sleep.

> Was he listening the
> whole time?

○ ○ ○

A few days later, the joyful young man came back to visit Woody. As he stepped out of the truck, Rooty noticed that he was wearing the white jumpsuit again. He also carried a small metallic box that had music blasting out of it.

After looking up at the sign, he climbed up the wooden staircase Carl had built the day after Woody was raised. Then he walked out onto the porous-metal walkway the men had installed the day before. The narrow walkway ran the full width of the sign. He jumped up and down on it a few times to make sure it was sturdy. Then he leaned up against Woody, peeled an apple with his jackknife, and ate it while he overlooked the park. Rooty could have sworn he was looking right at her.

The loud music had interrupted Woody's beauty sleep. "Rooty, who's blasting that music?"

"It's the guy that's been giving you the makeover. The funny-looking one," she replied.

"What's he doing?"

"He's just finished eating something and now he's heading back down the stairs." At that very moment, Rooty noticed that the pelicans were heading her way. "Woody, are you still thirsty?" she asked.

"Parched. Why? Does it look like it's going to rain?" asked Woody.

Rooty waved her branches, hoping to attract the pelican's attention. The nice one, with the yellow head, flew out of formation and headed her way. Not wanting to spoil the surprise, she motioned for him to come closer. When he did, she whispered, "Would you please serve my friend Woody some fresh water from the fountain near the hospital? He's had a rough couple of days, and he's really thirsty."

"It would be my pleasure, princess." With that, he flew over to the fountain, scooped up a bill full of cool water, and glided over to where the sign stood. Once he was directly above Woody, he dumped the water from his beak like an airplane putting out a forest fire.

"What the...who the..." said Woody.

What happened next defied explanation.

As Woody heard the pelican making his getaway, he asked Rooty, "Hey, why did that pelican just do that to me?" Before Rooty could respond, Woody shouted, "I can see! Rooty, I can see!"

Rooty could not believe her ears. *Did he just say what I think he said?* "Wait a minute, Woody. What do you mean, you can see?"

"What do you mean, 'What do I mean'? I mean, I can see! I can really see!"

"Are you messing with me again Woody?"

"No. Why would I pretend to see if I couldn't? Test me, if you don't believe me."

"Okay, how many branches am I holding up?"

"All of them," Woody said, laughing. "All of them. That's a good one, Rooty. You have to admit it, that's pretty funny."

Rooty was too shocked to laugh at her friend's joke. It was all happening too fast. Woody was changing right before her eyes. Not only could he see, he suddenly had a sense of humor. She'd never heard Woody laugh before, let alone attempt to be witty. *Is that really you, Woody?* she wondered.

"What's the matter, Rooty? Can't you take a joke? Don't you get it? Trees hold all of their branches up." Noticing that his friend was not responding, Woody altered the tone of his voice and his approach. "Rooty, are you feeling all right today?"

"I'm fine," Rooty replied, wondering where that question had come from.

Woody looked up at his friend's branches. Several of them were turning brown. "Are you sure you're feeling okay?"

"I'm positive. Why do you keep asking me that?"

"Well, some of your branches are turning brown. I thought maybe you were sick," replied Woody.

"That's normal for a palm tree, Woody. We shed our old leaves and grow new ones all the time. Let's forget about me for a minute and get back to the real newsflash. Woody, you can see! You can really see! What happened?"

The moment the question left her bark, she sensed the answer rising from her roots to her head. Rooty looked up toward heaven and whispered, "Thank you." She was convinced that she had just witnessed a miracle. *What else could it be?* she thought to herself. *There's no other explanation.*

"I'm not sure what happened. I'm much more interested in knowing what's about to happen!" replied Woody as the young man made his way back up the stairs and out onto the platform. "What's he got in his hand, and what's he planning to do with it?" Woody's voice was laced with panic.

○ ○ ○

The spirit filled young man began dancing around in front of Woody. He had what looked to be a small power drill, which was attached to a hose, in his right hand. The other end of the hose was attached to a machine that was humming. As he got closer to Woody, he started spraying something all over him.

Based upon Woody's reaction and his childlike laughter, it soon became clear that the young man wasn't torturing her friend; he was tickling him.

What's the right thing to do?

After watching the show for a few more minutes, Rooty asked Woody, "What is that stuff?"

"It's paint. Cool, tickly, new paint! Rooty, I wish you could try it. Trust me, I've been painted lots of times before, but this is different. Way different. It's almost like he's repainting my insides. It feels wonderfully refreshing and amazing. I feel like a whole new sign—like I'm brand new inside and out. Do I look as different as I feel?"

Rooty didn't want to lie, so she attempted to wrap the truth in a thin layer of sarcasm. "Yep, you look different all right—you definitely have a *hole* new look."

As the young man continued to coat the sign in paint, Rooty couldn't stop staring at Woody's holes. *How is he going to react when he learns the truth about his makeover?* she asked herself. Rooty faced a real dilemma. *I know good friends should be completely honest with each other, but if I tell him the truth he'll be devastated. What's the right thing to do?*

After giving it some more thought, Rooty decided the

timing wasn't right. She didn't see any point in breaking the bad news to Woody while he was having the time of his life. Besides, watching him being painted and listening to him laugh was boosting her spirits too. The more she listened, the more she thought to herself, *Too bad the Woody I'm seeing today can't stay forever. Now that would really be a miracle.*

Over the next few days, Woody and the young man drew a crowd. People stopped to watch the popular sign's transformation. Woody's laughter filled the air, causing the seagulls and gecko kids to take a closer look as well. One of the gecko kids got a little too close, a little too curious, and ended up with a white tail. His brother and sister couldn't stop laughing; neither could Rooty.

Woody's makeover was the talk of the town. The crazy young man was putting on quite a show and making Woody look better than ever. Woody was center stage, exactly where he wanted to be, and loving every minute of it.

Artie, the joyful young man had a flair about him that made people smile. The way he danced across the metal platform, high above the ground, waving his paint gun around was worth the price of admission. Between the Sun's rays and the wind, the paint appeared to dry and gloss over the moment it touched Woody's face. Rooty looked on as the young man finished covering every inch of the sign with white paint. Once he had completed his second coat, he took a quick lunch break.

Woody remained perfectly still, even though Artie was no longer painting his face; all except his eyes that is. They never stopped blinking. There was a good reason for this.

Woody didn't want to risk having his eyelids painted shut again. Now that he'd regained his eyesight, the truth about his past had become painfully clear too. Woody hadn't been blind to begin with, at least not physically speaking. The eyes in his head worked just fine now; however, the eyes of his heart needed some serious correction.

In the days that followed the pelican dumping water on his head, Woody realized that it was his outlook—his perspective on what mattered most in life that had cost him his vision in the first place. Woody hadn't lost his eyesight. Nobody had taken it away from him. He'd willingly traded it in exchange for success. Then one day, while celebrating all he had achieved, he just so happened to pick the wrong time to take a nap. Shortly after Woody drifted off to sleep, the shop owner stopped by to repaint him.

Having posed in the spotlight the night before he was exhausted. As a result, he ended up sleeping through the entire paint job, unaware he wouldn't be able to open his eyes when he awoke. Once his eyelids were sealed shut, and layer after layer of paint was added to maintain his image, he could no longer open them—even though he wanted to.

The irony of the situation was that very few people, if any, ever saw the sign at night. The shop owner added the spotlight as a security measure, not as a marketing ploy. He never asked Woody to work nights—that was his own choice.

Woody was still replaying the mistakes from his past in his mind when Artie hopped onto the platform and started back to work. The crowd returned as the young man began covering Woody with another layer of paint. This time he used a shade of blue that matched the sky perfectly.

Woody heard the people talking about "the blue sign" and thought to himself, *I'm blue all right, but not just on the outside. I can't believe I deliberately closed my eyes by day just so I could spend more time standing in the spotlight at night. What was I thinking?*

Once the blue coat of paint was complete, and the Sun and the wind had played their part by drying it, Artie began painting a giant circle onto Woody's face. It nearly covered the entire sign from top to bottom. At first, nobody could tell what he was making. It was just a large, beige circle. However, when he dusted it with a thin layer of white, one of the children shouted out, "It's a giant jelly donut. He's making a giant jelly donut!"

The boy was right. Artie was making a giant jelly donut, but not only was it giant, it was lifelike. The people couldn't believe how he had made an inanimate object appear to come to life. There was no doubt in anyone's mind that the spirit filled young man was a gifted artist. The way he blended the rest of the sign into the skyline was ingenious. For the most part it concealed the baseball-sized holes drilled throughout the perimeter of the sign. When Artie added shaded accents around the outer edge of the jelly donut, the result was a mesmerizing midair mirage. By the time he was finished, from the ground looking up, the three dimensional donut appeared to be floating above the buildings like a UFO.

Having finally finished his masterpiece, the young man made his way back down the stairs, stood in front of Woody, and evaluated his work. Just then, the Sun peaked between the buildings, like an industrial-sized spotlight. Since the Sun was directly behind the sign, his bright light practically blinded the people, making it difficult to see Woody's face. Artie and the crowd shielded their eyes.

The Sun was so bright that all that could be seen of Woody was his silhouette. As a result, when the Sun faded back behind the buildings a few minutes later, it appeared as though the sign had been unveiled. The crowd, in awe, broke out in spontaneous applause.

It had been a long but memorable day for everyone, especially Artie and Woody. As Artie packed up the tools of his trade and drove off, the crowd dispersed, leaving Woody alone to celebrate his new paint job and his "new lens" on life. He now realized that in the past, his quest for success had blinded him to the truth. At the same time, he knew that dwelling on the past, for too long, would rob him of his joy in the future. So, although he was ashamed of his past mistakes, he was determined to learn from them and move on. For the first time in many years, Woody not only looked great on the outside, he was beginning to feel good on the inside, too.

◦ ◦ ◦

Several days later, without warning, another storm approached town. With it, the wind came rushing back onto the scene too. "I see you're back on your post, little sign, but not for long," taunted Gusty.

Woody braced himself for battle while Rooty encouraged him just to ignore Gusty. However, that was easier said than done. The sign's memory of being knocked flat on his back made it difficult for him to heed her advice.

Meanwhile, Rooty took full advantage of the opportunity to steal another glance at the Sun. She cupped her branches and relaxed her trunk, allowing the wind to slam her forward and slightly to the right. "Wahoo!" she shouted as she reached her intended destination. As she looked at him she thought, *Wow, the Sun is even more beautiful when he's surrounded by dark clouds.*

An elderly couple entered the park and sat down on the bench below Rooty. She overheard the man call out to the couple from his car. "The woman on the radio just said, 'The people of Jelly Donut Junction have been advised to evacuate.'"

From that moment forward, the town buzzed with activity. All the people scrambled around as if they were squirrels preparing for winter. They moved everything inside the buildings, boarded up the windows, jumped into their cars, and sped out of town in a hurry.

"Wally, what does evacuate mean, and where are all the people going?" asked Rooty.

"It means to leave town," he responded.

"Leave town? Why would they tell everyone to leave town?" Woody asked.

Wally replied, in a somber tone, "I overheard the people inside of me say that the hurricane is heading straight toward us this time. Apparently, we're right in its path."

"What's a hurricane? And what do you mean we're in its path?" asked Rooty.

"It means—brace yourselves," warned Wally. "It means

we're in danger. I remember, when I was younger, a hurricane came through here and nearly ripped Bart's roof clean off. Fortunately for him, the Barber loved him enough to hire Carl to patch him up."

Before Rooty could ask her next question, Danny strolled casually out of the donut shop and headed in her direction. *He sure is different than the rest,* she thought to herself. *Everyone else is panicking and he's taking a walk in the park. What's his deal?*

Once Danny reached where Rooty was standing, he laid his hands gently on her bark, wrapped his arms around her trunk and squeezed. She had seen him do the same thing to Knotty the day before he fell. *What's he doing to me?* she wondered.

When he whispered to her, "Well, little tree, your time has come," Rooty really started to worry.

My time has come. For what? Is the storm going to be that bad? Rooty's mind conjured up images of Knotty lying on the flatbed truck as Trey hauled him off. Soon, she found herself consumed with fear, unable to shake the negative thoughts out of her head.

"Now that the sign is in position, we need to get you positioned too," continued Danny, in a gentle voice. "We need you to grow close enough to the Sun so that both of you can fulfill your role in *The Story.* For now, however, we just need you to survive this incoming storm. Remember to trust your lifelines, Rooty. There is no better anchor when the winds of change blow in."

Danny used his hands to search for one of Rooty's lifelines. Once he found the first one, he tugged on it to make sure it was secure. After testing the other three, he added, "They'll help you stand upright, little lady—good and firm." Danny sat down and leaned against Rooty. Then he pulled out a rectangular object and said, "Let me give you a little encouragement from *The Good Book.*" He spoke as his fingers felt the pages.

> There is a time for everything, a season for every activity under heaven.
>
> A time to be born and a time to die.
>
> A time to plant and a time to harvest.
>
> A time to tear down and a time to rebuild.
>
> A time to cry and a time to laugh.
>
> A time to search and a time to lose.
>
> A time to be quiet and a time to speak up.
>
> The Father has made everything beautiful for its own time.
>
> He has planted eternity in the human heart, but even so, people cannot see the whole scope of the Father's work from beginning to end.

Although Rooty didn't fully understand the meaning of what Danny read, she found the way he said it, and the rhythmic flow of the words, comforting. The anxiety she had previously been experiencing melted away as Danny read to her. His words echoed inside her head for the rest of the morning. Before long, she found herself putting them to music and singing them over and over again.

A few hours later, as Rooty reflected back upon her time with Danny, she thought to herself, *Danny was right. That is a good book. I wonder who wrote it? It sounds like the father, in that story, might be a gardener, like Trey down at the nursery.*

○ ○ ○

Rooty saw the Sun four more times that morning. After having dreamed of seeing him for so long, she wondered, *Am I getting better at bending with the wind or am I actually growing taller?*

Before long, the black clouds completely blocked her view, separating her from the Sun and making it impossible for Rooty to feel his presence. Instantly, Wally's words resurfaced, *"It means we're in danger."* The wind seemed to be angry with her. Gusty wasn't coming from one direction, he was coming from every direction. He blew so hard and for so long that Rooty wasn't sure if her lifelines would be strong enough to keep her securely anchored. She looked over to see how Woody was doing. Amazingly, he was not only standing, but Rooty could have sworn she heard him whistling.

Thwack, bang, thwap! One of the boards protecting Wally's front door sprung free and went sailing down Main Street. Rooty watched as it got vacuumed up into the sky and quickly drifted out of sight.

Over the next few minutes, nearly all of Wally's boards followed the path paved by the first one. Meanwhile, the sand from the beach pelted Rooty's bark like a jackhammer. Eventually, she found it too painful to keep her eyes open.

The last thing Rooty heard was Wally screaming, "Help me! Somebody help me!"

"Wally! Are you okay?" shouted the young palm tree, but it was no use. The old building couldn't hear her over the howling wind.

The louder Gusty got and the harder he blew, the tighter Rooty shut her eyes. She pleaded for the Sun to come back out, to drive away the clouds, to save her and her friends. Although the situation looked bleak, deep inside her heart Rooty believed that the Sun would eventually chase away the storm clouds and rescue them.

In the meantime, Rooty clung to her lifelines the way Danny had instructed her to. During the night, when the storm was at its worst, Rooty reflected upon the rhythmic words Danny had read to her earlier that morning. Doing so helped the time to pass more quickly and kept her mind off the storm.

○ ○ ○

That next morning, and every morning after the storm finally passed, Rooty celebrated life like she had never celebrated it before. That was the vow she had made to the Sun during the storm. She promised him that, if she survived, she would make the most of her life. To her, this simply meant being grateful for each new day and remaining faithful to her quest—to grow closer to the Sun. Rooty was totally committed to spending the rest of her days looking up, looking inside of her heart, and looking out for others.

The palm tree scanned the scene and was horrified by what she saw. The formerly quiet town looked like the center of a war zone. The ground was covered with debris. Cars were turned upside down. One of the tallest buildings behind the donut shop was missing it's top two floors, but there to her left, standing in the center of all the rubble, was Woody. Rooty's heart skipped a beat. She was overjoyed to see that her best friend was alright.

"Woody, you survived the storm. And surprisingly, your new paint job still looks great. How do you feel?"

"Stronger than ever, but I'm afraid Wally's in really bad shape—physically and mentally."

Rooty couldn't believe her eyes. All of Wally's windows were gone. Half of his roof was missing. His bricks were strewn all over the sidewalk.

"Wally, can you hear me?"

"Sure, kiddo. How are you doing this glorious morning?" asked the old building. His voice sounded weak. "Are you…are you…" He couldn't continue due to a violent coughing attack.

How am I doing this glorious morning? Woody was right, Rooty thought to herself. *Wally must be in shock.*

"See, I told you he was cracking up," blurted out Woody.

"I heard that, Woody" replied the old building before succumbing to another long coughing spell. When he finally recovered, he added, "I may not look great on the outside, but I'm stronger than ever on the inside, and what's inside matters most. Right, Rooty?" Having said his piece, Wally went back to his coughing spree.

While they waited for him to regain control, Rooty reflected on what he had just said to them. *I do feel stronger on the inside. I guess that's what Momma meant when she said "The wind makes your roots grow stronger." Why would stronger roots make me feel better on the inside?*

○ ○ ○

Why would stronger roots make me feel better on the inside?

The shop owner was the first to arrive back in town. He removed the boards from the door and windows before disappearing inside the shop. Over the next few hours, the rest of the locals came back into town, too, to survey the damage left behind by the storm.

The people who worked inside Wally everyday stopped by to visit him. An older man picked up one of Wally's loose bricks and replaced it before joining the others in front of the donut shop. Nobody could believe how much damage the storm had caused. Rooty listened as they discussed what they were seeing.

Some of the townspeople focused all of their attention on what was damaged. Others focused exclusively on all the things that had been spared. Rooty tended to feel more like the people in the second group, which included the shop owner, Artie, and Trey.

"At least we're all safe, and most of the buildings are in pretty good shape—all except for the old bank," said the shop owner. "But I'm sure he'll be okay in time."

"Hey look. Your sign is still standing," said a little girl with pigtails as she started skipping toward Woody.

The others followed her. As they got closer to the sign, Gusty reappeared and flipped a man's hat off, sucked it up into the air, and plastered it onto Woody's face. As the wind moved towards the beach, the hat fell onto the metal platform just below him. The little girl ran over, glided up the stairs, ran out onto the platform, and scooped up the hat. She paused for a moment to stare at the holes in the sign. Then she turned, waved to the crowd, and ran back down the steps to return the hat to its rightful owner.

Woody stared at the little girl during their brief encounter. He couldn't take his eyes off her smile and her brilliant blue eyes. When she looked up at him, he caught a glimpse of himself. It was like looking in a mirror. He wondered, *Are all children's eyes like hers? Do they all burn so brightly? Are they all so full of life?*

Even before Woody's eyes were painted shut, he'd never seen a child up this close before. *I guess that's one of the drawbacks of having such a lofty position,* he thought to himself. *Well, that's all behind me now.* Woody watched as the girl's father chastised her. Apparently, he wasn't too excited that she'd climbed up the stairs. He hoped the other parents didn't act the same way because he was looking forward to meeting more of the children.

As the people stood in front of the sign, the shop owner explained how Woody's makeover had come about. "When the last storm knocked him flat on his back, I called a meeting to seek wise counsel on ways to make the sign stronger. That's when my son, Danny, suggested drilling all those holes in him. He said it would make the sign stronger than ever."

He sipped his coffee before adding, "At first, I was skeptical, so I asked Danny to explain himself. He told me that poking holes through the sign would allow the wind to pass right through him. Ann, tell him what he said next."

"Oh, this is the best part," chimed in Ann, the architect, with a big smile on her face. "Then Danny said poking holes in him would make him 'a holey sign.'" She waited for the small crowd to finish laughing before continuing, "Danny also said that 'people will come, from miles around, just to see this "holy" sign play his role in *The Story.*'"

The people were confused by her second comment. They weren't sure if it was meant to be a joke or not. While they were trying to figure it out, the little girl who had rescued the man's hat grabbed her brother by the hand and made a beeline toward the stairs leading up to Woody.

The shop owner picked up where the architect left off. "It never ceases to amaze me how Danny sees things more clearly than we do; how he picks up on the things the rest of us overlook."

"Some day, I'd love to learn more about how he does it," said a young woman before turning to her friend and asking, "How does he do it?"

The donut man upon hearing her question said, "Well, perhaps today is the perfect day to start learning. Tell her how you do it, Danny," he encouraged his son. "Tell her what you told your mother that day in the park."

Danny, who didn't like to talk about himself or his giftedness, pretended not to hear the question as he made his way toward the stairs leading up to Woody. Enroute he overheard the little girl, who had rescued the man's hat, whispering to her younger brother. "Come on, Thomas. If you don't believe me, let's go up and you can see for yourself. Follow me." Fortunately, by the time they reached the stairs, Danny was waiting there to intercept them.

As they approached the place where the blind teacher was standing, the boy asked, "Mister, will you take me up, so I can touch one of the holes?"

"He doesn't believe they're real," added his sister. Danny stuck out both of his hands. Each child grabbed one, ready for their quest to begin.

Meanwhile, the shop owner, not wanting to miss an opportunity to influence others, said, "Well, I guess I'll have to tell you myself. When Danny was a young boy he told my wife that 'the blind see below the surface better; they see what's inside more clearly, because they're not blinded by appearances.' After watching him all these years, I'm convinced it's true."

Danny turned toward the crowd and said, "Things aren't always as they appear. That's why it's important to remember that—"

Those gathered, finished his sentence in unison. "...familiarity is the enemy of curiosity and life without wonder is a downer."

Danny was shocked. He'd been using that phrase for years, but he had never heard anybody repeat it before. *What do you know? They were listening after all,* he thought to himself. *Perhaps this storm is exactly what this town needs to finally come together.*

Danny, still holding the children's hands, desperately wanted to respond to the little boy's request, but he knew it would be too dangerous for him to navigate the steps. So instead, he raised their hands hoping to draw their father's attention. Within seconds he joined them. That's when Danny suggested that the boy's father be the one to lead the way up to the sign.

With a smile on his face and his son held proudly in his arms, the father carried him up the stairs and walked him out onto the metal platform. Woody watched the entire scene unfold right before his eyes. He listened to what the little boy said to his father as they got closer. "Katie said he really is holey. I don't believe her."

When his father raised little Tommy up to touch the sign, both of them grinned from ear to ear. The moment the boy's hand made contact with his face, Woody squealed, "Hey, that tickles." Apparently the boy couldn't hear him; he continued to caress Woody's face. It felt wonderful, but eventually Tommy got tired of touching the outside of the giant jelly donut and decided to poke his tiny hand right through one of the holes.

"Ooh, what did you just do?" asked Woody. "That felt really weird; not bad weird, just different."

Woody reflected on what he had just experienced. He couldn't really explain it, but it felt like the boy had reached right inside of him and touched his heart. His first thought was, *Wow, what Rooty's momma told her was true. The touch of a child's hand is an amazing thing.* Unfortunately, that uplifting thought was quickly dismissed when he heard the little boy say, "Daddy, look. The sign really is holy. It looks like someone whipped a baseball right through him. I can see right through these holes."

Woody had heard the shop owner talking about Danny's suggestion to drill holes in him. He had also heard the funny comment about him being a "holey sign." However, until now, he hadn't added two and two together to realize that he actually had holes drilled through his pretty face. *What have they done to me?* he wondered. *How bad do I look?*

Although he liked the extra attention, as the day went on and the wind continued to blow, Woody questioned Danny's recommendation to drill holes in his face. However, when one child after another climbed up to visit him, Woody experienced a change of heart. By the end of the day, Woody realized that Danny knew exactly what he was doing. *Hmm…who would have ever believed it,* he thought to himself. *Removing my mask and allowing others to see my flaws and imperfections didn't cause them to think less of me. It just made it easier for them to approach me. Go figure! I wonder if I've been looking at this whole thing backwards all these years.*

◦ ◦ ◦

What happened as the Sun rose the next morning can only be described as a miracle.

While another huge gust of wind whipped against the sign, the Sun poked through the clouds and cast his rays directly into Woody's face. Both the wind and the light passed right through Woody's new holes. Instantly the wind was transformed into enchanting music and the light into a glorious image. The children were the first to respond. They were mesmerized; frozen in place. All eyes were popping. All jaws were gaping. All fingers were pointing, but not toward the sign.

When Rooty turned to see what the children were pointing at she realized they were pointing at Wally. The moment she saw the marvelous image on his wall, she was spellbound too. By then most, but not all of the adults had tuned in to the spectacular show. Nobody had anticipated this moment. None of them could have except for Danny, who had predicted it from the beginning.

The image defied explanation. Rooty had never seen anything like it before. It was a dazzling mosaic of colors, brilliant and rich—a sight to behold. The sparkling image was overwhelmingly beautiful; yet she found it soothing to look at. The colors flowed together perfectly, yet each stood uniquely apart from the rest. *They are more vivid than I ever imagined colors could be; and most are colors I've never seen before.*

And that was just the beginning. The closer Rooty looked, the more she saw. The next thing she noticed was that each color had a unique movement. Some rotated clockwise, others spiraled counter-clockwise; none at the same speed or in precisely the same way. Still others flickered, whirled, or vibrated. No two were exactly alike. Apart from the spectacular colors, the movement itself was mesmerizing. *It seems like something or someone is in there,* Rooty thought to herself. *Whatever or whoever it is, is glorious.*

Ann, Trey, Carl, and the shop owner stood outside the donut shop discussing the old building's condition. They were waiting for the Sun to come up so they could inspect Wally when the miracle occurred. "Oh, my goodness. That is incredible," said Ann. No sooner had the words left her mouth than she remembered repeating Danny's prediction the day before. "This sign will be a holy sign that people will come from miles around to visit," she whispered to herself.

The shop owner stood closely by Ann's side. Close enough that he overheard what she had just whispered. If he hadn't heard the enchanting music with his own ears and seen the dazzling light show with his own eyes, he'd never have believed it. *I can't be the only one feeling this way,* he thought to himself. And he wasn't. He heard several other adults refer to the image as an optical illusion. They thought their minds were playing tricks on them, but they weren't. The looks on the children's faces convinced them of that.

Although not all who were present saw the image, for those that did the evidence was undeniable as the Sun's ray's filtered through Woody's holes and cast the glorious reflection upon Wally. The colors and the patterns in the design were so spectacular that they defied description. The beauty the people saw and the inspiration it provided them eclipsed their capacity to absorb it all. They were bewildered, stunned—awestruck. They were simply unable to wrap their minds around what they saw and experienced.

The fact that they didn't understand what they had just seen didn't stop them from believing they had seen it. However, it did stop those who didn't believe the image existed from seeing it.

For all of those people who believed that they had witnessed a miracle, some amazing things happened. Those who felt weary and overwhelmed suddenly felt refreshed.

Others who previously battled doubt and depression found themselves feeling hopeful and encouraged. Without exception, everybody who gazed upon the image using the eyes of their hearts instead of the eyes in their heads was changed from the inside out.

As quickly as the image appeared, it disappeared when a large white cloud swallowed the Sun. The image was gone. The people who had seen the image continued staring at the brick wall, hoping the glorious image would somehow reappear. But it didn't. No one wanted the experience to end, so they began comparing what they had either seen or heard. Those who hadn't seen or heard anything went about their way, ignoring all the hype; oblivious to the miraculous signs.

Before long, those who saw the image realized that no one had seen the same thing. Everyone had seen something completely different; yet none of them felt the need to justify or defend what they had seen. Nor did anyone have the desire to try to prove that what they had seen was better or more valuable than what the others had seen. Rather, everyone who had seen the image seemed fully content. Each person appeared satisfied that they had seen exactly what they needed to see. In the final analysis, all who had seen the image agreed upon one thing: *We all feel different inside—hopeful, joyful, and united.*

In the meantime, the sound of the enchanting music continued to flood the scene. It captivated, soothed, and inspired all those who could hear it. It was hypnotic, uplifting—joyous. Now that the image was gone, the music took center stage. It filled the hearts of the people. Again the children were the first to respond to it. They began dancing to the magical melody with reckless abandon. Eventually the adults, even those who claimed to have two left feet, followed the children's lead and began to let loose, seemingly uninhibited by their lack of grace.

It was a peculiar scene for those who hadn't seen the image and were unable to hear the music. From their perspective those who were dancing appeared to have lost their minds. Each person looked as if they were dancing to a different beat, yet none seemed to care. They were neither self-conscious nor critical of the way others danced.

All those dancing encouraged those who weren't to join in. Rooty and Woody, both enjoying the show from above, didn't want to disturb the party, so they just winked at one another and smiled. Rooty overheard one of the older children say, "Just follow your heart. Don't think about how to dance. Just dance. Listen to the music, find your groove, and dance."

Rooty noticed that those who were dancing never grew tired. Their energy seemed boundless. Furthermore she observed that their ability to stop themselves from dancing appeared to be beyond their control. It didn't look like they could stop dancing even if they wanted to. Some talked about stopping, but their legs refused to cooperate. Their brains no longer seemed to be in control of their bodies; they had been overridden by their hearts.

The young tree had never seen a group of people acting so crazy. By the same token, she'd never seen a group so accepting and agreeable. She listened to them as they discussed an even stranger attribute of the music, one that defied all logic. To a person they all agreed that the harder the wind blew and the faster it raced through the holes in the sign, the slower the music seemed to play. One woman, who was a music teacher, had this to say. "When the tempo should be accelerating, it is decelerating. I've never heard anything like it. More importantly, I'm not aware of any musician or instrument that could make such a sound. It defies the laws of physics. The harder the wind blows, the clearer, the more peaceful, and the more calming the music becomes. We could never reproduce that affect on the heart. Never, I tell you."

When the wind stopped blowing the music ended. But the laughter continued for some time. Those who had been dancing flopped to the ground. They didn't appear to be physically exhausted nor did it look as though they were gasping for air. They were just deliriously happy. One elderly gentleman grinning from ear to ear explained it perfectly. "We have seen remarkable things today."

As they lay there looking up at the sky, comparing what they had just heard, they discovered that some had heard lyrics and others had not. The music, like the image, somehow managed to identify and satisfy each person's unique desires and needs. Once again, everybody agreed upon one thing: *We all feel different inside—wonderful, light-hearted, and united by this experience.*

The shop owner asked, "Does anyone else feel like time froze, like the world stopped spinning for just a moment? Or that the past has somehow been forgotten?"

All nodded in agreement. Then Trey said, "It's like the present moment is the only one that matters."

"Exactly!" replied the music teacher.

Other adults chimed in too. Soon it was obvious that everyone who had heard the music felt exactly the same way—like time was more precious.

Meanwhile, one of the older children listening to the adults was thinking, *Here we go again; wasting time talking about wasting time. Why do adults do that? Too bad they can't just look at life the way us kids do. Oh well, their loss.*

Knowing he was not alone in his thinking buoyed the shop owner's confidence in his next statement. "Despite this catastrophic scene, despite all the external damage surrounding us, even though the evidence is undeniable, somehow deep inside my heart I feel like the storm never happened."

Again, all nodded. After that the small crowd remained frozen in place for quite awhile. Even the children sat fairly still and spoke only in their quiet voices. All seemed content to simply reflect upon the experience.

In the same way, Woody, despite everything the storm had done to him, found himself caught up in the joyous scene that unfolded all around him. So much so in fact that for the first time in many years, Woody was open to re-evaluating his approach to life. He began to realize that striving to project a perfect image wasn't the best way to live. *Working so hard to prove myself, to keep projecting an image takes way too much energy and leaves me feeling empty inside,* he thought to himself. *Besides, nobody wants to hang out with a stiff, boring old sign. I've got to stop taking myself so seriously and start enjoying life a little more.*

The ironic thing was that at the time, Woody had no

idea the Sun and the wind had used his holes to produce the enchanting music and project the glorious image. He just assumed the miraculous signs had come from another source.

Woody listened as the people talked about his make-over. One group was talking about his amazing new image, about how the artist had really outdone himself. Another was more interested in talking about his new holes. In part because he was curious, but mainly because he was still a little insecure, Woody was drawn to the discussion about his holes.

"I'm telling you, it's no different with that sign than it is with people. What he looks like on the outside has nothing to do with what we just witnessed," argued one man. "And everything to do with those holes."

"I agree wholeheartedly," chimed in the man's wife. "Just look at Harold here. Obviously I didn't marry him for his good looks, right?" She leaned over and kissed her husband on the cheek as the others enjoyed a good laugh.

When they had settled down, the woman continued her thought. "I married this big, old teddy bear because he has a good heart." With tears forming in her eyes she added, "What's inside matters."

That has a nice ring to it, thought Woody. *What's inside matters.* Woody repeated the catchy phrase to himself a few times to make sure he wouldn't forget it anytime soon.

Later that morning, after the people had returned to their homes, Woody made the most important decision of his life. He decided that instead of focusing on his external image, instead of worrying about his holes and imperfections, he would concentrate on trying to have a good heart. Although Woody still didn't fully understand how or why his holes had suddenly made him more popular than ever, the day's events had really transformed his thinking. Watching the people celebrate and listening to what they had said changed him from the inside out.

From that day forward, although Woody enjoyed his newfound popularity, he no longer felt the burning desire to pose for the spotlight, to project a perfect image, or to draw attention to himself. He still enjoyed his job, but he decided it didn't define him as a sign.

ꙩ ꙩ ꙩ

Over the next few days the town buzzed with energy and burst with enthusiasm. Everyone joined together and pitched in to clean up the debris left behind by the storm.

On the third morning, Rooty noticed a large crowd gathered in front of Wally. She overheard the president of the bank say, "Due to all the damage inflicted by the storm, we've been forced to close the bank temporarily until Ann can determine if the old building is safe for us to enter." Even though the bank was closed, the people just needed a place to gather so they stood around on the sidewalk outside discussing life.

Wally was the first to notice how the standard topic of conversation—making money and becoming wealthy—had fallen out of favor. Suddenly everyone who visited the bank seemed to be less concerned about making money and more interested in making sure their priorities were in order.

A small group of people had shifted their focus to discussing the meaning of life.

They were listening to some short guy going on and on about everyone needing to find their unique role in *The Story.* "We need to embrace each new moment and look beyond the current scene because there is a much bigger story unfolding all around us," he encouraged the others.

Storms sure have a strange affect on people, Wally thought to himself.

Wally nearly fell over when he heard what another woman had to say. "Whoever loves money never has money enough. Whoever loves wealth is never satisfied with his income." After spending fifty years as the only bank in town, Wally had heard everything there was to hear about people's outlook on money. If anyone knew the truth about money—how worrying about making it, spending it, and not losing it made people's lives worse, not better—it was Wally.

Not a day had gone by that Wally hadn't overheard some customer with lots of money complain about not having enough. From where he stood, they just never seemed to be satisfied with what they had. Yet others he'd observed, those who hardly had any

> Why do those who have the most money seem the least joy-filled?

money at all, celebrated life every step of the way. They never complained. They were always joyful, always hopeful, and appeared to be perfectly content. This always confused Wally. He'd never quite been able to figure out what he was missing. After all these years he still had the same question rattling around in his vaults. *Why do those who have the most money seem the least joy-filled?*

As he reflected upon these things, Wally's attention was drawn to one of the bank's wealthier customers. Wally recognized the woman immediately. He had been watching her for years. When she was younger, all she ever talked about was the next house, car, boat, or gadget that she was planning to buy. A few years back Wally learned that her husband had become very sick. Ever since that time, the woman didn't seem as talkative, but that was not the case this morning. She was talking a mile a minute.

Wally joined the conversation midstream, just in time to hear the woman say, "Yes, the same thing happened to us. The storm completely leveled our home. We've lost everything." Knowing that fact, and how much the woman cherished her possessions, Wally was shocked to hear what she said next. "Oh, well, it's only stuff. It's not like we can take it with us when we're gone, right? All that really matters is that my family and my friends are safe."

The woman continued sharing her story, but Wally's mind drifted. *Maybe this storm was a good thing after all. Despite all the damage it created, it appears to have changed the way people are thinking about life,* Wally thought to himself. *At least this woman has figured out there are more important things in life than money. Will the others be able to figure it out too?*

When Artie's truck rumbled into the circle a few minutes later, Wally noticed him first. "Hey, Woody, looks like your buddy is coming to visit you."

Woody was disappointed when the joyful young man drove right past him. He watched as the truck pulled into an open spot in front of the small park directly between Rooty and the donut shop.

Artie got out of his truck, closed the door, and walked towards Rooty. After crossing the street, he walked to where the blind teacher was sitting in the shade sharing *The Story* with a group of children. When Danny finished, the children from the hospital and a few of their parents peppered him with questions. While Danny patiently answered them, Artie tried to sneak up behind him.

Sensing the new arrival Danny turned and said, "You can do better than that. I heard you coming ever since you entered the traffic circle. You might want to try turning your radio down a few notches next time." Danny smiled as he stood up and met Artie with his standard greeting, a big hug.

The two men said goodbye to the children, walked over, and sat in the sand below Rooty. The younger man reached out and grabbed a hold of Danny's hand. Artie asked him to hold out his index finger and then he proceeded to use it like a pencil as he drew a series of symbols in the sand.

"Draw it again," whispered Danny. "A little more slowly this time."

The younger man wiped the original symbols away, like a student cleaning the chalkboard after class. Then, as Danny had requested, he borrowed his teacher's finger and traced the symbols slowly in the sand for the second time.

$$\dot{\alpha}\lambda\lambda\dot{\alpha}\ \ddot{\epsilon}\sigma\omega\ \lambda\acute{o}\gamma o\varsigma$$

"Where did you learn this?" asked Danny

"I didn't learn it. I saw it in the image the other day. Do you have any idea what it means?" The tone of Artie's voice was eager, not anxious. The symbols had been swirling around in his head for nearly three days. His heart was filled with anticipation. *I just hope he can crack the code. I know these ancient-looking symbols must mean something. I just wish I knew what.* Artie couldn't wait any longer. "Well, do you know what they mean or not?"

Danny leaned over and whispered something into the younger man's ear. Rooty strained unsuccessfully to hear what he said. Whatever it was launched the young man to his feet as he exclaimed, "It was all Greek to me, but I knew you'd know what it meant. I just knew it."

After giving the blind teacher a thank you hug, Artie added, "You never cease to amaze me, big brother. Somehow you always find a way to answer the tough questions, to unravel the riddles, and to solve whatever problems come our way. You always look past the scene and discover the unseen truth about things. I don't know how you do it, but I'm sure glad you do. What's your secret anyway? Nevermind, forget I asked that. No time now. Gotta run. You can tell me your secret later."

With that, Artie raced off towards his truck. He stopped halfway through the park and turned back toward Danny. He snapped a few mental pictures of the scene to capture the moment. Deep down inside he knew it was one he'd want to reflect upon again in the future. After filing the images away in his memory bank, he dashed off. Seconds later he jumped behind the wheel of the red pickup truck and sped off, leaving Rooty alone with Danny.

"Hello, Rooty, how are you today?"

"How did you know my name was Rooty?" she asked.

When he didn't respond she thought, *Perhaps he's deaf too. Wait a minute. He can't be deaf. If he was, how could he understand other people?* As she thought it through she realized that her mother had taught her to interpret people language, but Danny probably never learned how to interpret tree language. Unfortunately, Rooty had left the nursery before she had learned how to speak people language. *What a shame. I have so many questions. And from where I stand, Danny seems to have all the right answers lately. I sure wish he could understand me,* thought Rooty.

○ ○ ○

Barely an hour had passed when Rooty heard the familiar music blasting as the red truck made its way around the circle again. Artie pulled up right underneath Woody and emerged carrying the gun-shaped object he had used to paint Woody. *Now what's he up to?* wondered Woody. *My paint wasn't damaged by the storm, was it?"*

After taking a while to set up his tools, Artie gracefully added a series of large black symbols to Woody's face. Rooty noticed that they were different than the ones she could still see etched in the sand below her, but she sensed that they meant the same thing. A small crowd gathered around the sign again to see what the young man was up to this time. Within seconds of stepping onto the metal platform, Artie had finished what he started earlier. Woody's makeover was finally complete, at least from the young man's point of view.

Woody listened closely as two of the children standing on the ground below him tried to decipher the words. It was obvious that they were still learning how to read when an energetic mother stepped in to help them sound it out. Finally, having pieced all the sounds together, the children shouted it out to the rest of the crowd.

"What's Inside Matters!"

Artie, satisfied with his work, scooted down the steps and slipped into the shop to celebrate with a donut and some coffee. Outside the shop the townspeople had already begun wrestling with the meaning of Woody's new message. Some said, "It's referring to the powdered treasure inside the shop." Others said, "I'd rather have what's inside the bank, if it's all the same to you." Still others, especially a tight-knit group of donut shop regulars, said, "It's a sign from above; a reminder to all present that what's inside matters far more than people's appearance, occupation, or status."

Although this later group was small in number, they were a spirit-filled bunch. Each of them was committed to sharing what they called *The Good News* with others. Although they didn't realize it yet, in the coming weeks this faithful group would find themselves at the center of a controversial debate. Soon they would realize that they were being called to play a vital role in *The Story* that was unfolding in Jelly Donut Junction; to testify to what they had seen and heard—to defend their beliefs regarding the true source behind the miraculous signs.

○ ○ ○

Later that afternoon the architect and the carpenter met with Bill, the president of the bank. They stood on the sidewalk right in front of Wally discussing the damage he had sustained during the storm. Rooty and Woody listened anxiously as Ann shared her diagnosis.

"Sorry, Bill. I wish I had better news. We all want to save this historical landmark, but unfortunately the findings from the inspection report aren't good. The storm has left this building structurally unsound."

"So what does that mean?" asked Bill.

Ann, Carl, and Bill crossed the street and entered the donut shop, leaving the three friends alone.

Wally sensed his friends' deep concern for him. In an attempt to deflect the attention off of himself and his deteriorating condition, he said, "It's just like the people gathered in front of Woody were discussing earlier—*what's inside matters*. That's why you're not only a holy sign, Woody, you're a wealthy one too."

"How so?" replied Woody.

"You've finally found the hidden treasure, and now you get to spend the rest of your life sharing it with others and playing your role in *The Story*."

Woody had never heard Wally so excited about anything before. *Here he goes acting all crazy again,* Woody thought to himself. *He seems more excited about my future than his own.*

Rooty jumped into the conversation. "What exactly is Woody's role in *The Story?*"

"Let me ask Woody the same question in a little different way," replied Wally. "Who do you work for?"

Who do you work for?

Wally was a wise old building. Over the years, he had discovered the secret to influencing others by watching the blind teacher. Danny had proven that storytelling coupled with teaching others how to ask the right questions about life at the right time was the formula for serving others. Wally clearly understood the essence of becoming a great teacher, letting others draw their own conclusions.

"That's easy," replied Woody, without hesitation. "I work for the shop owner. He built me to serve a specific role in his business."

Wally reflected on his response before asking Woody, "Would you mind sharing with us what you think your specific role is?"

"My role is simple—to project an image. It's my job to draw people's attention to the shop." Woody's tone was very matter of fact. In the back of his mind he was thinking, *Isn't that pretty obvious by now?*

"Woody, let's shift our attention to Rooty for a moment, if you don't mind," said Wally. "Who does she work for and what do you think her role is?"

After an awkward silence Woody responded, "She doesn't work for anyone. She doesn't even have a job, as best I can tell. If she does, it's a well-kept secret. So, I guess what I'm saying is, Rooty doesn't have a role in *The Story*." The moment the words left his mouth, Woody wished he could retract them, but it was too late. He could see Rooty's branches spike up.

Rooty was more than offended. She was outraged. She was just about to give Woody a little lesson in diplomacy when Wally stepped in. "Woody, let's shift our focus back to you for a moment. Help me understand something. Are you saying one's role is defined primarily by who they work for and the job they are assigned to do?

"Yeah, I guess that's what I'm saying. How else could we define ourselves?" asked Woody, assuming a defensive posture. With a slight edge to his voice, he fired back. "Do you see it differently than I do, Wally?"

"Maybe, but I can't be sure until I better understand your entire view on the subject. Would you mind helping me think through it a little more?" asked Wally, totally diffusing the tension between him and Woody.

The shocked look on Woody's face convinced Wally that he was making headway. Although it was slow going, Wally pressed forward patiently by asking another question. "Woody, who does the shop owner work for?"

"Himself?!?" It was hard to tell if Woody was asking Wally or telling him.

"Are you sure?" asked Wally in a non-threatening manner before adding, "I would agree that it appears that way on the surface, Woody, but consider this. Sometimes we get so caught up in the scene, so buried in the demands and the harried pace of this world, that we lose sight of the bigger story unfolding all around us. That's why, unless we step back from the scene from time to time, it can blind us to the fact we're all here to serve a common purpose. In other words, if you think about it, you'll discover that we're all called to play a supporting role in *The Story."*

"A supporting role?" asked Rooty. "What is that?"

Knowing his days were numbered, and sensing that the time was right, Wally longed to share *The Story* with his two closest friends. In the past he had sprinkled a few scenes into their conversations, but he had never walked them through the entire story. Even though Wally was exhausted, he poured everything he had left to give into teaching his best friends the true meaning of life.

Over the next few hours Wally patiently explained how every person, place, and thing was created to revolve around the Sun; how each received its strength directly from him. Rooty and Woody listened closely as he shared how both of them had been custom designed, in advance, in order to play their unique role in *The Story.* Rooty understood this to mean that she and Woody were given a special set of gifts and talents that were intended to be used to serve others.

Toward the end of their time together, Wally said something that really touched Rooty's heart and encouraged her to more fully embrace her position inside the park. "So, as you can see, the Sun assigns each of us a specific place in the world. Then it's our job," the old building winked at Woody, "to work hard at reflecting his light, and his image, onto others."

So that's what Wally meant when he said, "We're all called to play a supporting role," Rooty thought to herself.

Wally concluded his invaluable life lesson by saying, "Always remember this: apart from the Sun, you can do nothing of lasting value."

"Let me get this straight," said Rooty. "Are you saying that Woody didn't project the image onto your wall, and that the Sun actually did all the work?" Rooty wasn't trying to be mean; she just wanted to clarify something, so she tried restating her question. "Are you saying Woody was just standing in the right place at the right time?"

"I guess you could put it that way, Rooty." Before Wally could finish his thought Woody's ego got the better of him.

"Wait a minute, you two. Are you saying I didn't contribute anything?" asked Woody.

"Woody, relax. I'm sure Rooty didn't mean that the way it sounded, nor did I. We're not putting you down, brother, we're simply raising the Sun up—and there's a big difference. Remember earlier when I said 'we all work for the same boss, serve a common purpose, and play a supporting role in *The Story*'?"

"Sure," replied Woody.

"Well, now you know the truth. All of our lives revolve around the Sun, and none of us can do anything of lasting value unless he stands behind our efforts. That doesn't mean we are worthless without his help. Rather, it means we're invaluable with it. Are you following me?"

Rooty and Woody both nodded, but their eyes were starting to glaze over. Wally, knowing he had given his friends a lot to digest, said, "I'm tired. So if you two don't mind I'm going to rest for awhile."

Wally closed his eyes. He had poured every last ounce of his energy into his friends. He was physically drained, but his heart was overflowing with joy as he closed his eyes and drifted off to sleep.

○ ⊃ ○

As concerned as Rooty was about her friend's future, it didn't stop her from celebrating life to the fullest. As the Sun peeked past Wally's damaged roof, the young palm tree was thankful for the pathway his misfortune had paved for her. Ever since Gusty had torn the right half of Wally's roof off, Rooty had been enjoying an unobstructed view of the Sun every afternoon. Although this allowed her to draw closer to the Sun than ever before, it was a bittersweet victory.

Knowing that her gain had come at Wally's expense troubled Rooty deeply. From where she stood, it just didn't seem fair that while she was celebrating her life, Wally was battling for his.

Why did it have to happen this way?

After wrestling with this question for several days, Rooty couldn't find any acceptable answers, so she decided to seek Wally's input. By the time she finally got up the courage to ask him, it was obvious that he was experiencing a great deal of physical pain.

Despite that fact, Wally's initial response reflected his selfless nature. "Rooty, I don't want what's happening to me to be a burden on you. I'm doing fine, really."

Tears flooded the young palm tree's eyes and began to flow down her trunk as she thought, *Could there be a better friend in the whole, wide world? He always puts others' needs ahead of his own. I hope I can grow up to be more like him someday.*

Wally, mistaking Rooty's tears and her silence as a

Why did it have to happen this way?

sign of sadness, set out to encourage her by saying, "Rooty, I am so proud of you and so grateful for our friendship. The first thing you need to know is that what you're feeling inside is completely normal. None of us like to see our friends suffer, especially when we're having the time of our life," said Wally.

"That's what's bothering me most," replied Rooty. "I wouldn't be having the time of my life if the storm hadn't ripped your roof off. Why does my joy have to come at your expense?" she asked.

"Ahh, now I see your dilemma. Rooty, listen carefully to what I'm about to tell you. Your joy didn't come at my expense. Joy isn't a scarce resource. It's not something we compete for. We don't give it to each other, take it from each other, or keep each other from getting it. Joy is a gift, Rooty, a pure gift that comes from a pure source—an unlimited overflowing, never ending source—the Sun."

After talking with Wally, Rooty no longer felt guilty. As a matter of fact, she felt energized, encouraged, and inspired. From that moment on Rooty celebrated each new day. She started every morning the same way, dreaming of the opportunity she would have later in the day to see the Sun face to face. On this particular afternoon as Rooty was enjoying her face time, and thinking about the way the Sun warmed her from the inside out, a large white cloud appeared on the scene, completely blocking her view.

Why does my joy have to come at your expense?

"Hey, get out of my way, cloud. Go away!" she hissed.

"What did I do to you, little tree?" billowed the overstuffed white cloud.

Rooty was startled by his response. She hadn't realized that the cloud could hear her. "I'm sorry, Mr. Cloud. I don't mean to be rude, but you're intercepting the rays I need to grow closer to the Sun, and that's what I live for."

"I know, Rooty, because that's what I live for too," replied the cloud in a gentle voice. "And please call me Fluff, okay?"

"Fluff, I like that name. Wait a minute, how do you know my name? asked Rooty.

"The Sun told me."

"You can talk directly to the Sun?" Rooty was confused. She had always assumed that the clouds and the sky were part of the backdrop, just part of the scene, not a living interactive part of *The Story.*

"Sure, we're very close. We talk every day."

"Then it's true? What my mother told me is true? Fluff, are you saying that if we get close enough to the Sun, we can talk to him and he will answer us?" inquired Rooty.

"Yeah. Why wouldn't he?" asked Fluff. "Does that surprise you, Rooty?"

"Sort of, but I know it shouldn't. So if that's the case, will you please move now? I only get to see the Sun for a little while each day before he moves behind the hospital or gets covered up by the…"

After an awkward silence Fluff finished her thought, "The clouds…before he gets covered up by all of us clouds. Don't worry, Rooty, we clouds hear that all the time. We're used to getting blamed for keeping others, especially people, from seeing the Sun. The truth is people can see the Sun through the clouds, even in the darkest, stormiest conditions."

Rooty had no idea what Fluff was talking about. When she subconsciously tilted, signaling her confusion, Fluff read her trunk language. "Rooty, let me take it a step further. You can see the Sun in the middle of the night if you want to. We can see him anytime we want to simply by closing our eyes."

"By closing my eyes? How would that help me see the Sun?" Then Rooty, assuming Fluff was pulling her root, began to laugh. "Fluff, you're funny. You really had me going there for a minute."

"Rooty, I wasn't joking. As I was saying, we always get blamed for keeping others from seeing the Sun. The truth be known, we can see the Sun better with our eyes closed than we can when they're open."

"You're not making any sense, Fluff. How can closing my eyes possibly help me see the Sun better?" Rooty asked.

"I know it sounds crazy, but when you close your eyes, all the things that distract you from seeing the Sun go away. Rooty, don't just take my word for it. Close your eyes for a minute and experience it for yourself," replied Fluff. "Trust me, Rooty, before you know it, you'll be seeing the Sun in your mind's eye whenever you want to."

"Seeing him in my mind's eye is not exactly the same thing as seeing him face to face," retorted Rooty.

"How do you know unless

How do you know unless you try?

you try? Go on, give it a shot," encouraged Fluff. "What do you have to lose? Besides, it's not like I can move out of your way any faster even if I wanted to. I'm not in control. The wind blows wherever it pleases, right?"

"If you say so," interjected Rooty. *How would I know how the wind works?*

"We hear its sound, but we cannot tell where the wind comes from or where it is going. As clouds, we have little choice but to follow. Speaking of following, in case you haven't noticed, even if I could move out of your way, my entire family is right behind me. It's going to be a while before you can see the Sun again anyway. So you might as well give it a try, Rooty."

What do you have to lose?

He's right. What do I have to lose? Rooty asked herself as she closed her eyes. At first she didn't see anything that looked remotely like the Sun. Her mind was restless. She was distracted by other things; she couldn't focus. Rooty still had her eyes closed when she heard Fluff, who was drifting farther and farther away, say "Keep trying, Rooty. I'll be back again soon, the wind permitting."

When Rooty opened her eyes, she caught a quick glance of the Sun before several of Fluff's family members blocked her view again. Not having any other choice, she closed her eyes, hoping to experience what Fluff had been talking about.

Over the next few weeks, with Fluff's help and encouragement, Rooty came to see the truth. She learned that *looking inside* was in many ways better than *looking up*.

Even on clear days when she could see the Sun, she realized how easily distracted she was by other things like seagulls, children playing in the park, and cars passing by. Yet, as Fluff had promised whenever she closed her eyes, the distractions faded away.

Over the next few weeks Fluff and Rooty spent a lot of time together talking about how life revolved around the Sun. Fluff's kindness changed Rooty's perspective on clouds. She no longer saw them as a barrier or threat to her happiness. Even on the windiest, cloudiest, and stormiest of days, Rooty found peace simply by closing her eyes and looking inside her heart. For Rooty, the ability to see the Sun no matter what made all the difference in the world.

From that day forward Rooty welcomed each day by closing her eyes and imagining herself talking with the Sun. Although she was grateful that Fluff had taught her how to see the Sun in her mind's eye, she couldn't stop thinking, *I still can't wait until I grow tall enough to speak with him directly.*

○ ○ ○

Rooty was wrapping up her morning quiet time, a time she devoted to thinking about all the Sun had done for her, when a black car pulled up in front of Wally. Ann, the architect, stepped out, carrying a circular yellow object. Rooty watched as Ann walked over to Wally's front door and wrapped yellow ribbon around the handles. Then she stretched the yellow ribbon all the way around Wally, fencing him in.

"What's she doing to you, Wally?" asked Rooty.

Before Wally could respond, Rooty overheard Artie updating Danny, "The old building has finally been condemned. Ann's over there right now putting up the yellow tape to keep the people from getting too close to him. I thought you'd want to know. Well, I gotta run. I'll catch you later, bro."

"Artie, don't forget to ask Ann to drop by for a visit. I have something I need to share with her," replied Danny.

Artie bounced across the street with his usual spirited strut. Rooty noticed that nothing ever seemed to get him down. A few minutes later he returned to the park with Ann. They joined Danny, who was sitting underneath his favorite palm tree. The three of them spent a good long while discussing the building, the people, and the future.

During their conversation Rooty learned a lot about life. She also discovered exactly what the word "condemned" meant. It meant that her friend Wally was very sick.

When Ann said, "We're not sure if we can save the bank," Rooty struggled to fight back her tears. She listened closely as Danny asked Ann a series of questions. His last question shook Rooty to the core. "So, are you planning to knock him down and replace him with another building?"

Unfortunately, some children were playing nearby. Their laughter drowned out Ann's response preventing Rooty from hearing it.

As the three stood up to say their goodbyes, Danny whispered something into Anne's ear while he gave her a parting hug. Whatever he said must have been good because it brought a huge smile to the architect's face.

"What an inspiring idea, Danny," she said. "You can

count on me to take good care of them." With that, Ann left Artie and Danny sitting under the tree and headed towards her car.

Based upon Ann's reaction Rooty assumed she had agreed to nurse Wally and some of the other buildings back to health. This thought boosted Rooty's spirits, but not for long. By lunchtime, the news about Wally being sick and Ann's plans to knock him down had spread throughout town.

The next morning several of the locals came by to visit the old building just before dawn. The shop owner joined them. He suggested, "Let's continue our conversation in the park, where the children will be safer." He sent one of the teenagers over to the donut shop with instructions to "bring a couple dozen donuts and some hot coffee back for all of us to enjoy. On the house."

The children played on the jungle gym while the adults gathered next to the benches in front of Rooty. They talked about the fact that Wally had been the center of town forever. They mentioned how he had seen a lot of change and weathered many storms. They even talked about how looking at the old bank caused them to reflect upon the past and contemplate their futures simultaneously. One man, who had just finished taking pictures of the old building, said, "He's protected every penny I've ever earned. I remember the first time my father—"

Suddenly, to everyone's surprise, the Sun rose, cast his light on Woody, and projected the image onto Wally's wall. As was the case with the first sighting, some saw it, some didn't. Those who saw it were frozen in place. All jaws gaping. All fingers pointing. Except for the children, that is, who immediately ran across the street, ducked underneath the yellow tape, and tried to touch the image dancing on the wall.

Unfortunately, before they reached the old brick wall, Fluff drifted in front of the Sun causing the image to disappear as quickly as it had appeared. The image hadn't been visible for very long, but that didn't stop the buzz about the miraculous signs in Jelly Donut Junction from spreading.

○ ○ ○

A few days after the second sighting of the image, hundreds of inaccurate reports, opinions, and rumors related to the events in Jelly Donut Junction flooded the scene. Of particular interest were the claims regarding the source of the enchanting music and the glorious image. The more far-fetched the claim, the more attention it got. It wasn't long before what had begun as a local event attracted national attention. Soon after that Jelly Donut Junction was swarming with reporters and camera teams seeking to be the first to capture the exclusive story.

Video shots of the children lining up to touch the holes in the sign and the old brick building looped in the background. It was a growing news story involving so many people, so many tales, and too many differences. Everybody put their unique spin on what happened that day. In the end, the media had their hands full. Trying to piece together what *really* happened, attempting to separate the tall tales from the truth, was a daunting task.

One of the more humorous moments came toward the

end of a live interview with one of the locals. After one gentleman had spun a most compelling and elaborate tale, his wife poked her head in front of the camera lens and said, "Don't listen to a thing he said. We weren't even in town that day!" But that didn't stop the man's story from circulating.

Danny made every effort to avoid the reporters. Not because he was afraid of sharing his opinion on what had happened, but because he didn't want to be in the spotlight. One day when a reporter finally caught up with him, Danny laughed, opened up the *Good Book* and said, "Here's my take on it. The words may be old, but they're as relevant today as they were the day they were written:

> When you see a cloud rising in the west, immediately you say, "It's going to rain," and it does. And when the south wind blows, you say, "It's going to be hot," and it is. Hypocrites! you know how to interpret the appearance of the earth and the sky. How is it that you don't know how to interpret this present time? Why don't you judge for yourselves what is right?

By the time Danny finished reading, the reporter was already halfway across the park. Rooty wondered why the reporter had walked away. *Perhaps he's already heard that part of The Story,* she thought to herself.

With each passing day and every updated media report, judging what was true became harder and harder to do. Fortunately, despite all the mixed reports, swirling rumors, and uncertainty, everyone agreed on one thing: they wanted to discover the truth about the source behind the so-called miraculous signs for themselves. And so over the next few months, people came from all over the world to see the signs. Some came hoping to catch a glimpse of the image. Others just really wanted to hear the enchanting music. The list of motivations for traveling to Jelly Donut Junction was endless as was the line of children seeking to touch the miraculous signs and eat the homemade donuts.

◦ ◦ ◦

The shop owner could barely make enough jelly donuts to keep up with the demand. His business boomed, but the boom came at a heavy price. Rumors about the donut man were spreading like wildfire. Soon many believed that he was the source behind a major ruse. They accused him of orchestrating the entire thing in order to sell more donuts.

Things only got worse when one woman told a reporter that Artie, the young man in the pickup truck, and Danny, the blind mystic, were related. "Not only are they brothers, they are the donut man's sons. Now what does that tell you?" inquired the incensed tourist. "This whole thing is a ruse."

When confronted with those allegations, the donut man laughed. "Sure they are my sons, but I don't see how that has anything to do with it. This is not about my sons. This is not about me, and it is certainly not about selling more donuts. You folks are covering the wrong story here. Trust me. You're interviewing the wrong source if you're looking for the real story surrounding the miraculous signs in Jelly Donut Junction. I encourage you to focus on the bigger story that is unfolding all around us. Unless we strive to look beyond the scene, what we can physically see and experience, we risk missing the Good News." With that, the shop owner concluded his comments and walked back into the donut shop.

His last statement only made him look guiltier to the skeptics in the crowd. They had already concluded that the Good News was just a cover up, a secret code that the donut man and his cronies in Jelly Donut Junction were proclaiming for selfish reasons. "They're all false prophets whose real motive is increasing their profits," accused one man.

Eventually the media's focus shifted to the old building. Several reporters cornered Ann and pressured her into admitting that Wally's impending demolition had in fact been delayed. "You pushed it back several weeks after the shop owner and others started proclaiming the Good News. Admit the truth, lady." That evening reports of the town council's plans to demolish the building upon which the image had been sighted became the talk of the town.

Rooty overheard a small group in the park discussing the breaking news. One woman said, "See, I told you 'the hole thing' was a scam. The fact they are trying to destroy the evidence proves it. I'm betting we'll find hidden speakers next. We've heard the last of the enchanting music and seen the last of the image. I'm sure of that."

By the next morning the entire town had reached a tipping point. The tourists were upset because they felt hoodwinked, and the townspeople started to take sides as well. The shop owner sat in the corner booth reflecting upon everything that had happened. *First the storm comes and unites the townspeople. Now in the midst of these spectacular miracles, the Good News is dividing us. Why is this playing out this way?*

By lunchtime, tourists and locals had decided. Everyone quickly fell into one of two camps: those who believed in the signs and those who didn't. To make matters worse, some folks started name calling, referring to each other in their conversations as "believers" and "non-believers."

Why is this playing out this way?

Not everyone fell cleanly into one group or the other. Several of the believers lost hope. One said, "Without the wall to catch the image, we'll never see it again." Those who never believed in the signs to begin with, the most convicted of the non-believers, proclaimed, "The Good News being spread by the believers simply isn't true. The music and the image never really existed. It's nothing but an elaborate hoax to bring more tourists to town so they can profit from the crowds."

Thanks to the extensive media coverage, soon after the news of the old building being demolished hit the airways, people stopped coming to see the signs. Unfortunately almost all of the tourists had concluded it was a hoax. As a result, by the end of the year the number of people visiting Jelly Donut Junction and the donut shop was at an all-time low.

Despite all the doubt and uncertainty swirling about town, the terminally ill children in the hospital across from the park never lost hope. They still wanted to touch the old building. They were drawn to him, and, in turn, he drew his strength from them. Wally was overjoyed.

Like Woody, he had never experienced the touch of a child before all this happened. He cherished every moment, welcoming each new child as they approached. The old building couldn't stop talking about how special each one of the children was and how special they made him feel. Wally and Woody compared stories of what each of their first touches felt like and how the children's enthusiasm had re-energized them and rekindled their childlike sense of wonder.

In the meantime, Rooty felt left out. Although she hated to admit it, she even felt a little jealous of her friends because she longed to experience her first touch from a child. Every day the children from the hospital gathered around Danny. While they breathed in the fresh air, the blind teacher entertained them with stories and led them in inspiring sing-a-longs. Their laughter echoed throughout the park, and their smiles reflected the hope they felt inside: the hope of getting better soon—the hope of a child. All of them believed that one day soon they would hear the enchanting music and see the image for themselves. In the same way, Rooty hoped that one day the children would be drawn to her so she could share in their joy and experience what her friend Wally was experiencing.

For a long time the children's hope buoyed the townspeople's desire to see the image. Soon however, those so-called believers who hadn't actually seen the image for themselves began to doubt that it had ever existed. This doubt triggered a cascading effect even amongst the believer's camp, proving that doubt is the deadliest of viruses. Not just because it spreads so quickly within the body, but because it attacks the spirit too. Within days, doubt had infected the entire town. Even some of those who had seen and heard the signs began to lose hope.

Eventually most of the townspeople returned to their normal routines, rarely taking time to stop, look, and listen for the miraculous signs and wonders. All, that is, except for the core group of believers who frequented the donut shop. They remained hopeful and committed to playing their role in *The Story.* They never lost hope. They never stopped believing that what they had seen was real. They never stopped spreading the Good News.

○ ○ ○

After the crowds were gone, Rooty overheard Ann and Eddie discussing Wally's fate right in front of the old building.

"It's time," Ann said. "Eddie, we just can't afford anymore delays or any more media coverage. I'll meet you and your demolition team here first thing in the morning." Following a long sigh she added, "I'd like to get this old building knocked down before anyone has a chance to protest. Oh, and one last thing. You haven't forgotten the promise I made to Danny, right?"

"No, Ann, I haven't forgotten and my team is all set. We'll be here before dawn," replied Eddie. "Boy, this place just won't be the same without this building, will it?"

"No, it sure won't, Eddie." Ann shook her head. "I've never had to knock down a building before, and I sure hate having to start with this historic landmark."

She was still shaking her head as the two headed for

their cars and drove off, leaving Rooty to wrestle with what she had just overheard. *How can this be happening? Why doesn't the Sun stop it?* Rooty's mind drifted back to the conversation Ann, Artie and Danny had recently had in the park. The very one in which Ann appeared to promise to take care of Wally and the other buildings damaged by the storm. *If Ann didn't promise to protect Wally, what did she promise Danny?* wondered Rooty.

The young tree wept as reality sunk in. She now understood, for the first time, the true meaning of the word condemned. Rooty now knew it was a terrible word. *It means the final judgment has been rendered. It's too late for anybody to save Wally now.* Rooty's branches drooped as she completed her thought. *His life, his future, and our friendship will end tomorrow morning.*

Wally's situation frustrated and confused Rooty, especially since she knew how hard she and Woody had prayed for him to recover. Rooty had seen many children and adults closing their eyes and praying too as they stood in front of the condemned building. *Wally really seemed to be responding to the prayers and the attention he was getting from the children,* thought Rooty. *I was convinced that he was going to recover. I'm afraid I was wrong...about everything,* she thought as she cast a desperate glance upward hoping to see the Sun. When all she saw were gray clouds she wailed, "Where are you when I need you most? Why aren't you listening to me? Why aren't you helping me? Momma said you would always be here for me. I guess Momma was wrong."

"Rooty, are you talking to me?" asked Wally.

Rooty was too embarrassed to admit the truth. Besides, the last thing she wanted to do was add to Wally's heavy burden. "No, Wally. I was just…I was just—"

"What's wrong, Rooty? You seem upset. Do you want to talk about it?" asked Wally.

Wally's continued concern for Rooty, given his impending death, defied comprehension.

Wally hasn't complained about his situation once, not one time has he sought sympathy from others during his entire ordeal. Too bad his roof isn't as strong as his heart, thought Rooty to herself before asking, "Wally, how can you be worrying about me when Ann is planning to…when they are going to…" Rooty couldn't hold it together any longer. She burst into tears. Tiny droplets fell from the tips of her branches.

After giving his friend a moment to recover, Wally completed Rooty's sentence for her, "…knock me down in the morning. Is that what's upsetting you, darling? Please don't worry about me. I'm doing fine."

"How can you be so calm? Aren't you afraid?" Rooty, detected the desperation in her own voice and realized how selfish she was being. *How can I be focusing on my own needs when—*

Wally interrupted her thought when he asked. "Rooty, have you already forgotten everything we've talked about?"

"Well, umm, no…I—"

"You're just upset, Rooty. Calm down and think for a second about everything your momma taught you. Reflect on everything we've talked about over the years." Wally gave her a moment to reflect before adding, "I know that you know the answer to your own question because I remember listening to you teach the exact same lesson to Woody recently. Do you remember what you told him that day right after he got knocked down?"

Rooty hesitated while she tried to recall the specific lesson she had taught Woody. *I remember telling him not to worry about future storms or about how he would get back onto his post. Then I told him that the storm would make him...that's it!* "I remember now, Wally," said Rooty.

"Good. I knew you would. How about sharing that invaluable life lesson with me?" encouraged Wally.

"I suggested that the storm would actually help Woody grow stronger. Then I taught him the same way Momma used to teach Knotty and me." Rooty demonstrated, holding up two of her branches while saying, "Stop asking, 'Why is this happening *two* me?' and start asking, 'Why is this happening *four* me?'" By the time Rooty finished her sentence she was holding up four branches instead of two. "That's how it works, Wally. You turn two into four, and it shifts your entire perspective on life."

"Well said, Rooty...and that's exactly what I've done. See, you've answered your own question. I knew you could do it," Wally added.

"Yes, but your situation is completely different," appealed Rooty.

"How so?"

"Woody was only temporarily knocked down. In your case it's going to be permanent. I'll never see you again, Wally." Her voice cracked and faded as she began to sob.

"Rooty, please don't lose heart. Even though on the outside I'm falling apart, on the inside I am at peace. I've lived a great life. Remember, things aren't always as they appear. This is just a temporary condition. So don't get so focused on the current scene that you miss the bigger story unfolding right before our eyes."

Rooty did not respond. For the next few minutes she stood completely still. Wally, assuming she was processing what he had just said, knew that nothing he could add at this point would help. Deciding that it wouldn't be the best time to introduce a new lesson, he simply whispered, "I need to get some rest now, Rooty. We'll talk some more later, okay?"

Rooty was too distracted to respond. *Wow, I guess there's a big difference between teaching a life lesson and living one out. Wally does both. He's really something special. I'm going to miss having him around.*

◦ ◦ ◦

When the people stopped coming to Jelly Donut Junction, the children started asking questions.

Why didn't those people hear it? Why didn't they see it?

Since some of their parents were amongst the non-believers, their questions went unanswered. Eventually, when the children didn't get the answers they were seeking from their parents, they found someone else to ask them to. Fortunately, in this case they went to the right source. Over the next few

Why didn't those people hear it? Why didn't they see it?

weeks story time in the park with Danny became a popular event.

With some help from the volunteers at the hospital, Danny set up a show-and-tell experience to help the children discover for themselves the answers they were seeking. The turnout was amazing. Children from both the hospital and the town joined in. Rooty had never seen so many children visit the park at the same time. It was a heart-warming sight.

Once all the children were gathered together, Danny began his lesson. First, each child was given a clay pot and asked to decorate the outside. Each of them went about this task a little differently. Some used special markers, others applied stickers, but most used paint.

Rooty thought the painters were the most fun to watch. She noticed that they fell into two groups. The first used brushes, energetically slapping what looked like flowers and colorful rainbows onto their pots. The second, consisting of a small group of boys, decided not to use brushes at all. Instead they stuck their hands directly into the paint then covered not only their pots but also their faces and clothing in a mosaic of color.

When the children finished, Danny asked the volunteers to bring the children over to where he was standing. While they had been busy decorating their pots, the volunteers had emptied a few bags of dark rich soil onto the ground. Danny invited the children to sit underneath Rooty with the mound of dirt filling in the center of their circle. Rooty noticed the pile looked just like the dirt the men had used to secure Woody's new post.

Once the little ones were settled, Danny opened up the Good Book and read them a story, his fingers skimmed across the pages as gracefully as the words flowed from his mouth.

A farmer went out to sow his seed. As he was scattering the seed, some fell along the path; it was trampled on, and the birds of the air ate it up. Some fell on rock, and when it came up, the plants withered because they had no moisture. Other seed fell among thorns, which grew up with it and choked the plants. Still other seed fell on good soil. It came up and yielded a crop, a hundred times more than was sown.

Danny stopped, closed the book and pulled a bag of seeds out of his pocket. "Who wants to sow some seeds?" he asked.

After the volunteers filled each of the children's pots with soil, being careful not to disturb the wet paint, they helped them plant their seeds. Then they watered them while Danny continued teaching, "So, do you think your seeds will grow?"

"Yes, as long as we water them," responded one of the girls.

"What else will they need to grow?" asked Danny.

"Sunshine," shouted out another.

"Very good. But what do you think would happen if we just dropped the seeds into the pot without any soil?" asked Danny.

"That's easy," the children responded, the jumbling of

their voices revealing their subconscious need to compete for Danny's attention.

"They wouldn't grow because they're just like the ones dropped on the path in *The Story*," interjected one of the children before the others could get the words out of their mouths.

"Right again. You children are very wise. You're good listeners too. See if you can find the answer to this next question. What would happen to the seeds, even those planted in the good soil, if they never got any sunlight?"

This time all the children chimed in together. "They wouldn't grow either."

Danny, convinced they understood how the seeds needed good soil, water, and sunlight to grow, moved on to explain the deeper meaning of *The Story*. He pointed out that each child, like the differing pots, was unique in their individual design and appearance. He encouraged them to celebrate the fact that no two of them were exactly alike. Then he compared the good soil to their hearts. He concluded the show-and-tell by saying, "The seeds of hope, desire, wonder, and joy have been planted in your hearts. That's why you can see the image and hear the enchanting music. As long as you keep those seeds in the Sun's light, they will never stop growing."

The children all clapped. It had been a great day in the park. Satisfied that the children finally understood that *what's inside matters,* Danny had a volunteer lead the children back across the street and into the hospital.

Rooty, who had been listening all afternoon, wondered, *Am I planted in the good soil?* After thinking about it for awhile, she wasn't sure. This left her feeling slightly unsettled. *I sure hope Trey planted me in the good soil, but what if he didn't?* she wondered.

> Am I planted in the good soil?

o o o

Wally slept all the way through his last night, leaving Rooty wondering if she would get a chance to say goodbye to him. Now, shortly before sunrise, she called out to him, "Wally, Wally, wake up."

The old building struggled to open his eyes. "Good morning, Rooty. How are you feeling today?" he asked.

Like we're running out of time, she thought to herself as she shrugged.

Wally, as if he could read her mind, asked, "Rooty, do you remember the day Danny came out of the donut shop and told you your time had come?"

"Yes. How could I forget that? Danny really scared me that day," she replied.

"Do you remember the words he read you from *The Good Book?*" asked Wally.

"I sure do," replied Rooty. After replaying the little song she had created in her mind she added, "I remember them, but I'm still not sure I know what they mean."

"I thought that might be the case. Be patient, you will soon enough." As the Sun peeked over the horizon, the old building asked Rooty to wake up Woody. Then he asked her to call her other friends together in the park. "There is something I'd like to share with all of you before I go," he said.

Rooty called out to Woody; to Sammy the seagull, who was sleeping on top of Woody's post; and to the pelican passing by. She enlisted Sammy and the pelican to carry out Wally's request. A few moments later all were gathered. They sat in silence, even the gecko kids—their collective faces reflected the respect they had for the old building.

"Why the long faces?" asked Wally. "Today is a day of celebration, not sadness. My life is not ending, it's just beginning. You all need to—" The rumbling of several large yellow vehicles entering the circle drew everyone's attention.

A chill ran down Rooty's trunk followed closely by the gecko kids, who were running for cover.

"As I was saying," continued Wally, "you all need to remember, things aren't always as they appear." Wally continued speaking, but Rooty and the others were unable to hear him over the noise made by the oncoming vehicles.

Ann's car pulled up first. She and Eddie emerged from the car wearing white hard hats. Eddie, armed with an orange flag, directed the large vehicles into position before giving them the signal to cut their engines. Rooty and her friends welcomed the silence as Ann led Eddie and his demolition team across the street and into the donut shop.

○ ○ ○

"We don't have much time." said Wally. "Rooty, can you please recite the words Danny shared with you? I want everyone to hear them."

Rooty was amazed at how clearly she remembered the words and how easily they flowed from her mouth.

There is a time for everything, a season for every activity under heaven.

A time to be born and a time to die.

A time to plant and a time to harvest.

A time to tear down and a time to rebuild.

A time to cry and a time to laugh.

A time to search and a time to lose.

A time to be quiet and a time to speak up.

The Father has made everything beautiful for its own time.

He has planted eternity in the human heart, but even so, people cannot see the whole scope of the Father's work from beginning to end.

When Rooty finished, all eyes were fixed on Wally. He stood firmly and courageously as he spoke from the center of his heart. Unfortunately, he had much to say and very little time to say it in. After spending several minutes answering questions about the meaning of life—after encouraging each of them to find their role in *The Story*—Wally paused for effect. He wanted to end by reminding all those who were present not to get too caught up in the scene. "So remember to keep looking up, looking inside your hearts, and looking out for one another."

As the engines roared back to life, Rooty asked Wally,

> How will we know when we've found our role in The Story?

"How will we know when we've found our role in *The Story?*"

Before the old building could respond, a large metal ball hit his back wall, sending a tremor through his entire foundation. His time had run out. As Wally fell, he whispered, "Goodbye, my friends. I love each of you. Take care of each other. I'll see you in heaven."

Those gathered were not the only ones in Jelly Donut Junction who cried that day. All the people who had worked inside the building cried too. Others were concerned Wally's departure meant that they would never see the image again. Now that Wally was gone, nothing stood between the sign and the ocean to reflect the image. But no one was sadder or missed Wally more than Rooty.

Danny, having anticipated this moment and knowing how important it was to keep the people's hopes alive, had already initiated a plan. Rooty would soon discover what Ann had really promised to do that day in the park. Ann stood by a pile of bricks, guarding each from the demolition crew. Every brick from the wall the image had first appeared upon was in that pile. Danny had asked her to preserve the original canvas, hoping it would reunite the townspeople.

Moments after Wally was no longer standing, while the dust was still settling, Danny emerged from the donut shop and met Ann on the sidewalk. After borrowing a megaphone from Eddie, Danny addressed the crowd. "This old building meant a lot to all of us. He touched each of our lives. If you would like to take a brick home to remember him by, please step up."

Danny personally handed a brick to each of the townspeople. He asked them to take it home and put it in a special place. With each brick came a reminder. "This brick is a symbol of our hope in the future. Although Wally is physically gone, our memory of him will last forever."

The blind teacher's gesture was well received. It had only taken a few minutes for the wall on the old building to disappear, but now, brick by brick, his legacy was being carried forward in the hearts and minds of the townspeople. *We have not seen the last of you, my friend,* Danny thought to himself as he carried off the final brick. *You will not be forgotten, I promise you that.*

○ ○ ○

Rooty slept later than usual the next day. Watching Wally get knocked down had taken a toll on her. She had nothing left to give—physically, emotionally, or spiritually. Her branches hung limply against her trunk, her roots and her head felt heavy. Both were physical signs of how she felt on the inside—heartbroken. The thought of turning two into four couldn't have been farther from Rooty's mind. Although she tried several times to open her eyes, she couldn't. She wouldn't.

Losing Wally, her friend and mentor, turned the young tree's world upside down. So much so that for the first time since leaving the nursery, Rooty's desire to grow closer to the Sun was gone. Her interest in speaking directly to the Sun had wandered off as quickly as the bricks from the old building. *What's the point?* she thought. *It certainly won't bring Wally back.*

Rooty began to question everything, including whether the Sun had ever really cared about Wally or her to begin with. Her typical joy-filled spirit vanished. Not only did she feel the deep loss of her friend and mentor, she felt like the Sun had abandoned her too. It was a dark day. Rooty made it even darker by dwelling on the past and refusing to open her eyes to the promises of a new day.

When Rooty finally opened her eyes later that morning, the clear view of the beach startled her. *Wally really is gone.* She watched the waves roll in one after another; nothing could stop them from reaching shore. In the same way, nothing could stop the questions from rolling through her head. *Where were you when I needed you most? Why didn't you listen to me? Why didn't you help Wally?* Nothing she thought or did stopped the questions from rolling in. Unfortunately, at least from her perspective, the answers were nowhere in sight.

The longer Rooty stared at the ocean and the harder she tried to find the answers, the more distant she felt from the Sun. The more distant, the emptier she felt inside. The emptier she felt inside, the greater the distance appeared between her and the Sun. It was a never-ending cycle. There was no doubt about it; losing Wally had cast Rooty into uncharted territory. She had woken up in an unfamiliar scene.

Rooty was quickly slipping into a dangerous downward spiral. Fortu-

> Where were you when I needed you most?

nately, just before she hit rock bottom, when her hope and her future seemed to hang by a thread, Rooty heard a voice calling her name. "Rooty. Rooty, can you hear me?"

At first Rooty thought Woody was calling out to her, but when she looked over at him she realized he was taking a nap. So Rooty looked all around the park, only to discover there wasn't anybody standing nearby. At that point, she assumed the stress had finally pushed her over the edge for good.

Again, she heard someone calling her name. *I must be imaging that voice,* she thought, but she wasn't.

"Rooty, why aren't you answering me? I know you can hear me."

This time the voice seemed clearer and closer. "Yeah, I can hear you, but I can't see you," she replied.

"Rooty, do you believe in the Sun?"

Convinced that someone was playing a trick on her, Rooty decided to play along. "Who is he, sir?" she asked sarcastically. "Please tell me so that I may believe in him."

Rooty scanned the sky expecting to see Fluff approaching, but there wasn't a cloud to be seen. It was perfectly clear; there was nothing there—except for the Sun. Normally having a clear view of the Sun would have excited her, but not today. She quickly looked away and closed her eyes.

"You have now seen him; in fact he is the one speaking with you," continued the voice. "Now open your eyes, Rooty. Look at me. Believe in me. I've been here all along. I never left you, and I never will. I'll always be with you as long as you believe in me."

Rooty opened her eyes and looked up at the Sun. Instantly, her anger melted away. So did her earlier feelings of being abandoned. Within seconds she felt like she was being pulled up out of the darkness. She felt loved, re-energized, hopeful—more alive than ever before.

"I'm sorry I ever doubted you. I do believe." Rooty took a deep breath before adding, "Please forgive me."

"I already have, Rooty," replied the Sun. "I forgave you before you were ever planted in the good soil."

Rooty couldn't believe her ears, nor could she have been any happier. Discovering that she in fact had been planted in the good soil buoyed her spirits. She spent the entire morning talking with the Sun. Then, she dedicated the rest of the day to reflecting on their conversation. *How can the Sun, who watches over all the earth, not only know me by name, but be able to take the time to intercept my thoughts too?* she wondered. *How is that possible?*

Despite her desire to live a life rooted in faith, Rooty had always doubted when her mother and Wally told her that the Sun knows us better than we know ourselves. Now she knew, beyond a shadow of a doubt, that they weren't exaggerating one bit. They were simply speaking the truth.

○ ○ ○

At first, Rooty found the thought of the Sun looking *at* her and reading her thoughts a little unsettling, like he was spying on her—waiting for her to mess up. But over time, she found the thought of him looking *out* for her comforting, like having a guardian angel watching over her. Once she began seeing the Sun in this new light, her desire to draw closer to him grew stronger than ever. Over the next few weeks she awoke each morning eager to spend time with him.

On most days, simply knowing he was up there, whether she could see him through the clouds or not, filled her with a sense of peace that surpassed all understanding. Today, however, was not starting out to be one of those peace-filled days.

Before Rooty even had a chance to open her eyes and stretch her branches, before the Sun's first light ever appeared in the sky, Woody called out to her. "Rooty, I'm worried about you."

"About me?"

"Yeah, I've noticed that you're still not making good use of your days."

Rooty found Woody's comment offensive, but before she could respond he continued his thought, "I should have said something before now. Wally was right. We all need to find our role in *The Story*—especially you. Don't worry, starting today, I'm going to help you find your groove."

Rooty was shocked. Woody's perception was so far off base that it rendered her speechless. *Wow, talk about having a blind spot. If anyone should be worried about finding their groove it's you, pal,* she thought to herself.

After taking a deep breath and biting her tongue, Rooty replied, "I appreciate your offer, Woody, I really do, but I'm good with my life. I already feel like I've found my groove, like I'm doing exactly what I was created to do."

This is going to be harder than I expected, thought Woody before asking, "How do you figure? Are you saying you were created to stand around, stare at the Sun, and talk to yourself? Be honest with yourself, Rooty, let's face it, that's all I've seen you do ever since I've known you. You haven't changed a bit since Wally went away."

"I haven't been talking to myself. You may have regained your eyesight, but you might want to check your hearing."

Before Rooty could set the record straight, three large trucks wedged themselves between the sign and the tree like riot police dispatched to bring peace to a hostile scene. Within seconds there was a flurry of conversation and activity. Surprisingly, none of it came from Rooty or Woody. That's because the two of them were too busy trying to figure out what was happening. They watched as four men jumped out of the first truck with shovels in hand and marched directly toward Rooty.

o o o

When Rooty saw the tree doctor coming around the circle in his flatbed truck a few minutes later, she was convinced the men had come to take her away. *But why? Am I sick? I don't feel sick.* Her mind raced. *Even if I am sick, can't you just give me some medicine?*

Trey, as if he could read Rooty's mind, approached her, carrying a cordless drill.

"Ouch!" she screamed as he punched four holes through her outer bark. He punched one on each side and sunk them deep into her trunk. When he finished drilling the last hole, instead of giving her medicine, he just walked away. Rooty watched as Trey headed across the park and handed something to Danny who was sitting alone on a bench in the shade.

Just then, one of the men tied a rope around her trunk while a second man, holding the other end of the rope, pulled it tight. Rooty's imagination got the best of her. *They're going to pull me over. Then they'll haul me away on the flatbed truck just like they did to Knotty. Why is this happening to me?*

Fortunately, Rooty quickly realized her imagination had led her astray. The man didn't intend to pull her over. He was only using the rope as a guideline to paint a white circle around her base. Rooty briefly lost visual contact when the man disappeared behind her. By the time he reappeared to her left, Danny and Trey were standing directly beneath her. She had been so distracted she hadn't heard them approach.

Something about having Danny and Trey nearby relieved her. When Danny wrapped his arms around her trunk, it brought to mind the last time he approached her in this manner right before the storm. *Remember, things aren't always as they appear,* she thought. Still she couldn't help but wonder, *Has he come over to say goodbye?* Fortunately, Danny wasted no time in establishing the purpose of his visit.

"Rooty, I am so proud of you. Trey's been telling me that you've grown much closer to the Sun. I can only imagine how majestic you must look by now. You must be a sight to behold when you are swaying in the breeze. Trey and I were just talking about how all the people look up to you as they pass through the park. You're going to make an amazing centerpiece for our new fountain."

Danny pulled out a handful of tiny black granules from his pocket. Then Trey guided Danny's hand, helping him gently press several granules into each of the four holes that Trey had drilled into her trunk moments earlier. When they were finished Danny looked up at Rooty, as if he could see her face, and smiled.

The sounds of shovels breaking through the roots of the grass startled her. "Remember, no digging beyond this white circle because we don't want to damage her roots," said Trey as he stood guard over the treasure buried inside of the line.

"What are they doing to you?" asked Woody. He had been trying to get Rooty's attention ever since the trucks first appeared on the scene because he wanted to finish their conversation.

"They're building a fountain around me," beamed the palm tree. "I'm going to be the centerpiece."

"Great, a centerpiece," said the sign sarcastically. "Now can we get back to our discussion? Can we focus on helping you find your role in *The Story* before your branches swell any farther? A centerpiece, *hmmph*—you need to find your center before you can be a centerpiece," he mumbled.

"I heard that, Woody. What's wrong with you today? You're acting like you're jealous. Remember, we're not competing for joy. There is plenty to go around; it's not a scarce resource. You should be helping me celebrate the fact that someone is finally recognizing my gifts and acknowledging my contribution to this town."

"Contribution, that's a good one," blurted out the sign. "You haven't lifted a branch or contributed a thing to this town since I've know you. You're wasting whatever gifts you were given because all you ever do is stand around—"

Rooty had heard enough. "Look who's accusing whom of standing around."

"Well, at least I'm standing around by design, unlike somebody I know. Perhaps you've overlooked the fact that I was created to stand around, to project an image. Oh, yeah, and in case you didn't notice, I was the one who projected the image that brought everyone together. I'm the one who put Jelly Donut Junction on the map. If anyone should be the centerpiece around here, it should be me. I deserve it. Not some little tree who spends all of her days laughing with the seagulls, giggling with the geckos, and dreaming about talking to the Sun. Oh, but wait, I suppose you're going to tell me that's the role you've been cast into. Am I right?"

"I hate to burst your bubble, Mr. Holy Poser, but there is a big difference between having holes drilled in you and being *holy*. You still don't get it do you? You're not blind anymore, but you still can't see. Truth be told, you haven't changed much since you were saved. Deep down inside you're still the same old self-centered sign. You might be fooling other people, but you're not fooling me," barked Rooty. "You're still trying to project an image, and you know it."

Rooty was on a roll. There was no stopping her now. "Woody, it wouldn't surprise me if you're still taking full credit for projecting the image. In case you've completely forgotten what Wally taught us, let me remind you. It was the Sun's image that reflected off of Wally, not yours. All you're doing is standing there. You're just available for the Sun to use as a filter. Remember, you can't do anything without him," barked Rooty.

"I should have known you would redirect this back to being my problem. I'm well aware of my role and of the fact that without the Sun, I'm just an insignificant sign. The question remains: When are you going to figure that out for yourself and start taking life seriously? When are you going to find your role in *The Story* and start spending time on purpose? When are you going to realize that you still have to do something? Or do you just expect to stand there looking graceful while you wait for the Sun to do all the work?"

"That's exactly what I expect to do, Woody, stand here gracefully and gratefully, unlike some people I know who try to steal the Sun's spotlight," replied Rooty.

○ ○ ○

Rooty spent the rest of the day, and a sleepless night, thinking about her squabble with Woody. It really upset her, and part of her regretted mixing it up with him. She knew the way she had acted was wrong; the things she had said were hurtful. The way she was judging Woody was simply unacceptable. At the same time, part of her felt like she hadn't done anything wrong. *Somebody needed to set the record straight,* she told herself. *Somebody*

Why do I always have to be the one to apologize?

needed to help Woody open the eyes of his heart so he could see the truth.

Rooty wrestled with the idea of forgiving Woody and apologizing for her rude comments, but she just couldn't find the strength to do it. *Why do I always have to be the one to apologize?* she thought to herself. As the Sun rose to usher in a new day, Rooty muttered to herself, "Besides, he started the whole thing to begin with. It wasn't my fault."

"What wasn't your fault, Rooty?" asked Fluff.

Rooty hadn't seen her friend the cloud in quite awhile. Right off the bat she noticed how much closer he looked than when they first met. *I really have grown a lot closer to the Sun,* she thought to herself.

"What wasn't your fault?" Fluff asked a second time.

"You wouldn't understand," replied Rooty.

"Try me," he encouraged.

Rooty began explaining the situation to Fluff this way. "Woody's newfound popularity has gone straight to his head. Now he's acting like he's risen above the rest of us. He acts like he has it all together and the rest of us don't." Rooty paused before making her most important point. "Oh, did I mention he is still taking credit for projecting the image onto Wally?"

Fluff listened patiently. When Rooty was finished, he said, "So basically, Woody's head is stuck in the clouds and that's bothering you."

Rooty was amazed at how quickly Fluff grasped her situation, at how well he understood her concerns. Sensing he had earned her respect, Fluff took the opportunity to share the truth from his vantage point above the scene.

"Rooty, I've noticed this happens to all of us—trees, clouds, and people too—at various times in our lives. Things start going our way, we achieve some level of success, and the next thing you know we begin talking down to others. We start acting like we have all the answers.

"Nobody's exactly sure what causes us to behave this way. Some say, 'The thin air at this elevation impairs our thinking.' Others believe it's hard to stay grounded with so many people looking up at us. I guess an overdose of admiration can leave us thinking more highly of ourselves than we ought to. Regardless of what causes our inflated view of ourselves, the result is the same. Looking down on others damages our relationships. Nobody understands that better than us clouds. That's why whenever I catch myself drifting off course, I just remember what my mother taught me."

Rooty wished Woody was awake to hear what Fluff was saying. She felt like he needed to hear this lesson way more than she did. "What did she say, Fluff?"

"My mother taught me two things I'll never forget. First, she always used to say, 'Remember, it's not about you, Fluff. Everything, I mean everything—on the earth, under the sea, and in the sky—revolves around the Sun. Including you. Don't ever forget that.'"

"Wow! That's exactly what Wally told Woody and me before he...before he..."

Fluff could see that Rooty was still deeply grieved by the loss of her friend, so he waited for her to regain her composure.

"Anyway, Fluff, I know each of us only plays a small role in a much bigger story, but Woody doesn't appear to have grasped that concept yet. He still acts like he is playing a bigger role than he really is. He seems oblivious to the fact that we're all playing a supporting role in *The Story*."

Fluff held back his smile as he listened to Rooty vent. It was clear to him that her head was in the clouds too, but he didn't want to lose this teachable moment. "So, you understand your role, right, Rooty?"

"Sure."

"How about my role? Is it clear to you too?"

> Now who's got their head in the clouds?

Rooty, looked a bit perplexed. "Absolutely. You provide shade and make it rain."

"You're only half right. I don't make it rain, ever. I'm not that kind of cloud," said Fluff.

"There are different kinds of clouds?" replied Rooty.

"Yup, just like there are different kinds of trees. We each play a unique role. I'm more of a decorative cloud. I was created to draw people's attention upward. When they look up at me, eventually they end up catching a glimpse of the Sun."

"That's all you do?" The moment the words left Rooty's mouth she caught herself. *Now who's got their head in the clouds?* she thought to herself. Although it was never easy to admit she was wrong, Rooty knew Fluff was right. Even though she hadn't intended to, she was guilty of looking down her trunk at Woody—of judging him unfairly.

Fluff could tell by the remorseful expression on Rooty's face that his mother's lesson had hit the target. Knowing Rooty was quick on the uptake, he asked, "Do you want to hear the second thing I learned from my mother?"

"Sure, unless you think it will go right over my head." Rooty's laughter was a good sign. It cut through the tension in the air and put both her and Fluff at ease.

"No worries. Momma always told us kids that this lesson is a matter of the heart, not the head," said Fluff.

"Why did she say that?" inquired Rooty.

"I guess it's because it will make you *feel* better than you *think* it will." When Rooty didn't respond to Fluff's play on words, he moved forward. "Anyway, Rooty, here's the lesson: forgive to forget—*give* your apology, so you can *get* to feeling better. In other words, apologizing from the heart benefits the one who's giving the apology more than it does the one receiving it."

Fluff's words hung in the air as the wind gently blew him away. His lessons touched Rooty's heart and transformed her way of thinking. It was a humbling experience at first, but soon she embraced the fact that she still had a lot to learn about life.

Accepting Fluff's advice with her head was the easy part. Putting it into practice with all of her heart would definitely be the hard part. Although Rooty knew she had some apologizing to do, she wasn't looking forward to forgiving to forget. In fact, she wasn't sure she'd be able to forget how Woody had treated her, even if she managed to forgive him.

○ ○ ○

Rooty and Woody were immersed in a deep conversation when the trucks pulled up the next day. For the first time in the history of their friendship, each was able to really share what was on their mind. Unfortunately they weren't finished when the men with the shovels showed up to finish digging the circular trench around Rooty. The hole was nearly waist deep and, at least from Woody's perspective, didn't look much like a fountain. *How can they call it a fountain if it doesn't even have any water?* he wondered.

Ann, Trey, and Carl sat directly underneath Rooty. Their feet dangled off the edge of the firmly packed chunks of dark earth that protected Rooty's precious foundation, looking over the blueprints for the fountain. The palm tree's lifelines had been removed and now her roots alone held her up. This no longer concerned Rooty because she knew her roots were firmly planted in the good soil. Furthermore, she knew deep down inside that she wasn't standing on her own anymore. She could see Danny, Ann, and Trey watching over her and she certainly could feel the Sun's presence.

Trey looked up and said, "When you guys are finished digging, Carl needs help building the frame for the new bank's foundation. Ann wants to start pouring the cement as soon as possible."

"Ann, how long will it take to raise the new building?" asked Trey.

"We'll have the outside done in a few months. The inside will take a little longer to complete," she replied.

"Isn't that always the case?" Trey smiled as he put his arms around Carl and Ann and guided them towards the edge of the trench. Rooty and Woody watched as the three hopped into the trench, crossed over to the other side, climbed out, and headed into the donut shop.

"Rooty, you're going to make a beautiful centerpiece," said Woody.

"Thanks, Woody. It sounds like we're about to have a new neighbor pretty soon too. Are you excited about having a new canvas to project the image upon?"

"You betcha, and I can't wait to meet him. But I really miss Wally, don't you?"

"Oh, Woody, I miss him terribly. Not a day goes by that I don't think about what happened to him," replied Rooty as tears welled up in her eyes.

Woody, hoping to cheer his friend up before drifting off for his daily nap, decided this was the perfect time to unveil his hidden treasure, a well-kept secret. "Well, if it's all right with you, Rooty, we need to get some beauty rest."

"Speak for yourself, you old sign. I'm wide awake. Besides, there can only be one centerpiece in town, and the job's already taken."

The two friends burst out laughing.

"Rooty, I'm so glad we had this heart to heart. We both know it wasn't easy for you to be the first to apologize after the way we must have sounded the other day, but there is still one thing we need to tell you."

"Why do you keep saying we?" asked Rooty.

"Take a closer look. Do you notice anything different about us?" Woody was grinning from ear to ear.

"You mean besides the fact that you're acting stranger than ever? Nope, nothing looks different to me."

Do you notice anything different about us?

"So, what you're saying is, I'm not the first

sign you've seen wearing a leafy green wig? And I suppose the fact that I've been growing taller doesn't strike you as a little odd either? I wouldn't recommend she become a detective anytime soon, would you, Knotty?"

Rooty was speechless. It took a long time before the reality of the scene playing out right before her eyes sunk in. At first she was in shock, but then she was overjoyed. So much so that she could barely breathe. Knotty was back. *Actually, he never left. He's been hidden in plain sight all along.*

She shook her head in disbelief. *My cousin is alive and well. Not only that, but he's lifting Woody up. Who would have ever believed that my stubborn cousin would end up playing a supporting role? He's gone from wanting to stand firmly on his own, to standing firmly attached to Woody. Things sure do have a funny way of working out sometimes.* Rooty looked up at the Sun, knowing he had been working behind the scenes again. "You're amazing," she whispered to herself.

"Hello, cuz. You look more beautiful than ever," said Knotty in a gentle voice.

"And you look stronger and more firmly rooted than ever," replied Rooty.

Something about Rooty's own words immediately triggered a flashback. She was transported back in her mind to the worst day of her life—the day Woody and Knotty both lay lifeless on the ground.

Rooty closed her eyes and strained to recall the words Danny used that day which renewed her sense of hope. It took her a while to sift through her archives, but she finally located what she was looking for. *At least there is hope for a tree: If it is cut down, it will sprout again, and its new shoots will not fail. Its roots may grow old in the ground and its stump die in the soil, yet at the scent of water...*

"That's it! That's what happened!" shouted Rooty.

"What's what happened?" asked Woody and Knotty.

"Woody, do you remember the day my pelican friend gave you that unexpected shower?" asked Rooty.

"How could I forget it? That was the day I regained my sight; the day I received a new lens on life," responded Woody enthusiastically.

"Exactly. That was the day. And it was the water that revived Knotty," said Rooty.

"What do you mean it revived me?" asked Knotty.

"That was the day your new roots sprouted. The storm destroyed your old roots, but with Trey's help, the Sun gave you a second chance. In a way it's like you were born again, Knotty. I am so glad you're back."

The sincerity in Rooty's voice evoked an immediate response from Woody. "We are so blessed to have each other, to share a common role in *The Story,* and to have you watching over us, Rooty. Thanks for all you do, pal. We love you."

"Yes, we are, Woody," added Knotty. "Yes, we are. Rooty, your faith has kept us together all these years. Thanks for laying your heart on the line for us."

Rooty closed her eyes and pondered the overwhelming sense of joy she felt deep inside. She felt deeply loved and fully appreciated by her friend, the sign, for the first time in the history of their friendship. *I remember Momma used to talk about all the incredible blessings that flow from the fountain of forgiveness, but never in my wildest dreams would*

I have imagined that a cloud would be the one to show me how to tap into that source, thought Rooty.

"I'll catch up with you guys in a little while," said Rooty who sensed that she was on the edge of unlocking an important life lesson. She closed her eyes and wondered, *Where would I be without my momma and friends like Wally, Trey, Fluff, Danny, Woody?* Rooty stopped making her list as she realized that for the first time ever, she and Woody were seeing eye-to-eye; not just physically, but spiritually too. *Knotty may never grow as tall as me, but we're both growing closer to the Sun.*

Then Rooty started a new list. *Who helped Woody change? Was it Trey, Danny, the Shop Owner, Fluff, Artie, the yellow headed pelican and…the Sun?* Tears of joy rolled down her trunk as the life lesson unveiled itself. Rooty connected the dots in her mind. *And who helped Knotty come back to life after his fall?*

As Rooty reflected on her last question she realized that the Sun had used an ordinary cast of characters to play a supporting role in each other's lives. Finally, the life lesson appeared front and center. *We're all in this together. Each of us is called to play two supporting roles, not just one. In addition to using the position we've been given to reflect the Sun, we are called to serve one another; to help others get in position, too.*

Later that day after Rooty finished sharing what she had discovered with Knotty and Woody, Woody added, "Well, I think we learned another invaluable lesson today."

"What's that, Woody?" inquired Rooty as she leaned closer.

"We learned that we shouldn't judge one another, because despite our innate differences, despite where we are born, how we were raised, or what we look like on the outside—we're all exactly the same on the inside. And what's inside matters, right?"

"Right!" chimed Knotty and Rooty in stereo.

With their differences behind them, Rooty, Woody, and Knotty spent their days growing closer to the Sun, serving others and enjoying their unique roles in *The Story*. Each devoting, in his or her own way, their time and talent to helping others discover that the hidden treasure is all too often hidden in plain sight—*what's inside matters*.

o o o

Over the next several months life was good, especially for Rooty. She now stood at the center of the renovated town park, like a crown jewel on display for all to see. The original fountain next to the children's hospital had been transformed into a spectacular waterspout, which formed the source of the graceful stream that fed the pool surrounding Rooty. The water, after creating a dazzling, rhythmic show for the children, cascaded gently down a manmade channel before disappearing underneath the street. When it emerged on the other side, it ended its journey in the pool that encircled Rooty. Then a series of pumps filtered it before piping it back to the source.

The sound of the flowing water and its enticing sparkle were irresistible to the children, which in turn made it difficult for the parents to keep them out of it. A wall outlined the pool, creating a bench for people to relax upon and a barrier to keep the children out of the water. On really hot days, the children darted in and out of the waterspout near the hospital, but the parents never allowed any of the children to even dangle their feet in the pool surrounding Rooty. This was a major source of frustration for her. She so badly wanted to experience the touch of a child. Now it was doubtful that she ever would.

Another thing that proved to be challenging for the parents was trying to keep the children from picking the beautiful flowers lining both sides of the fountain. The children's desire was fueled by the fact that they thought the flowers were still theirs. You see, after Danny's show-and-tell lesson in the park, he encouraged each of them to donate their creations to the park. Most of them did and the volunteers arranged their clay pots in a breathtaking display beside the fountain.

Banks, the new building, was nearly complete. A few weeks earlier, when Banks' outside was being framed, Rooty concluded that he was going to block her view of the Sun. By the time Banks' grand opening arrived, Rooty had accepted the fact that no matter how tall she grew, she would never be able to see the Sun over her new neighbor again. Before long, however, she was reminded of the same old lesson: *Things aren't always as they appear.*

Even though Banks was much taller than Wally had been, he actually improved Rooty's ability to see the Sun. Unlike Wally, whose exterior was made of brick, Banks' walls were made out of mirrored glass. As a result, from sunrise until mid morning, Rooty could see the Sun's reflection in Banks' windows. But this still left Rooty facing a dilemma for the rest of the day. As much as she enjoyed seeing the Sun's reflection during a time of day where she typically wouldn't have seen him at all, she longed to see him face to face again.

As Rooty shared her concern with Woody, he asked her, "Aren't you the one who taught me how to turn two into four?" After pausing for effect, he added, "Yeah, that was you. And if I'm not mistaken...no, I believe I have this right. You were the one who taught me to close my eyes, so I could see the Sun whenever I wanted to—even at night."

Rooty's best friend had played his role. He had gently reminded her to look beyond the scene, beyond her circumstances, and to make the best of every situation. Rooty took a moment to regroup. *The truth is, I can't see the Sun directly anymore, but I can see him more often than I used to be able to. Woody's right. The Sun is right there on Bank's shiny face during the morning hours. The rest of the time I can close my eyes and visit with him using the eyes of my heart. Why didn't I think of that?*

Unfortunately, the townspeople didn't appear to be as willing to accept the new building as Rooty was. Instead of seeking ways to embrace Bank's differences, they seemed intent on pointing out his flaws. Worse yet, they kept comparing him to Wally, which was nothing more than a waste of energy. Those who had seen the image, or those who were hoping to see it for the first time, were the worst offenders. From their perspective it appeared that between the sign being raised up higher each day, and the changes in the texture of the walls, the odds of seeing the image again were stacked against them.

Of course, that was before two teenagers who were sitting on the bench outside the post office spotted the image a few months later. Ironically, after all of the fuss and concern over Banks' ability to provide a suitable backdrop to capture the image, he never got a chance to try. According to the teens, a large tractor trailer making its way around the circle intercepted the image before it ever reached the new building.

At first, they thought they were imagining it. However, when the truck stopped at the intersection, it became obvious to them that its sides were plain white. Apparently that's when they realized the brilliant colors and personal messages they had just seen must have come from another source.

Like the others who had previously seen the image, both saw something different. Yet even though they only saw it briefly, each had seen exactly what they needed to see in order for their hope to be fully restored. Rooty listened closely as one of them told a reporter, "My sense of wonder has been restored, my entire perspective recast, even the way I think is different now. I feel completely transformed, like I've been turned inside out."

Despite this enthusiastic report by the teenagers, very few people believed that the image had returned to Jelly Donut Junction. A few days later the locals gathered around the fountain to share their concerns. "All you're going to do is create another disruptive and debilitating media blitz," protested the crowd.

It was obvious, at least from the hardcore believers' perspective, that most people remained skeptical and doubtful. Their doubts seemed to center around two issues. First, they challenged the decision to anchor the sign to a palm tree. "Whose obscure vision was that anyway?" one woman tossed out. "Eventually the sign's post will either grow too tall or become too skinny and frail to properly support the sign. By then, if it doesn't topple over, it will cast the image right over the building."

The second concern voiced by the people was related to the new building's ability to capture the image. "It will pass straight through the glass wall, or reflect off of it into deep space. Either way, we'll never see it again," said one man. Still others didn't believe the teenagers actually saw anything on the truck to begin with. "They're just a couple of kids seeking attention, looking for their fifteen minutes in the spotlight."

After a lengthy debate, Trey and Ann, who had been huddled off to the side strategizing with Danny, stepped up onto the wall of the fountain to address the people of Jelly Donut Junction.

Trey was the first to speak. "Calm down, everyone. We have a few things to share with you that might eliminate your immediate concerns. First, although the sign's post is in fact a member of the palm family, it's a completely different type of palm tree than the one in the fountain. Therefore, it's nearly reached its maximum height. In the future it will only grow slightly wider, not taller—ensuring that the sign will remain in its current position for many years to come."

Rooty winked at Woody, who winked back. Knotty joined in by lifting his branches to signal victory. The three friends had really learned how to celebrate life and appreciate their differences. They couldn't imagine getting any better news. It looked like they would be together for the foreseeable future.

Having captured the people's attention, Trey looked to Ann, who added, "As far as the building is concerned, the image won't pass through the glass, and when it banks off of it, we will capture it for all to enjoy. This building was designed and constructed to serve this specific role. We planned for this moment from the very beginning." Ann paused for a moment to make sure she still had everyone's attention before asking an important question. "How many of you still have the brick Danny gave you at home?"

Most everyone raised their hands. Those who didn't were either new in town or had chosen not to take a brick home to begin with.

"Great. We're really going to need to rally together if we expect to pull this off. I need all of you to help spread the word," encouraged the architect.

Ann went on to explain how Danny had made her promise to carefully set aside and guard all of the bricks from the old building. "It wasn't until after Danny stepped in and gave them all away to you folks that I realized I'd been assigned the impossible task. I wasn't able to protect any of them."

"That's not true, Ann," interrupted Danny. With a grin like a Cheshire cat he added, "Unless what you're saying is you didn't protect the one I gave to you." Suddenly every eye and every ear was trained on the blind teacher. Ann was not put off; she and Danny had rehearsed this transition in advance.

Trey and Ann helped Danny up onto the wall. He turned to the crowd and read them a story from *The Good Book*. It was an inspirational story about an ordinary man, Nehemiah, who led an extraordinary group of townspeople who faced the greatest test of all—discouragement...loss of hope. They faced a daunting task; through perseverance and faith they rallied together to rebuild the wall to their city. While the blind teacher read, the people of Jelly Donut Junction hung on his every word.

When Danny finished, he said, "Now, just like Nehemiah, we're going to rebuild our wall."

"Let us start rebuilding," shouted one man enthusiastically.

"Do you really think you can bring the wall back to life from a heap of bricks?" challenged another.

"I know some of you may think we're wasting our time. I understand if you don't believe building a wall will make any difference, so if you don't want to help, don't help. However, please consider this—regardless of what you think about our vision or whether you're planning to help us execute it, we need all of you to bring your bricks back tomorrow morning. We're going to need every last brick, including yours, Ann, if we're going to achieve our goal."

Over the next few days, with Danny's encouragement to keep the faith, the townspeople brought back every single brick. With Ann's help, they used the bricks to build a memorial wall dedicated to Wally. At night while the people were sleeping, Ann, Trey, Artie, and the Shop Owner finished the wall and covered it with an old awning from the donut shop. The next morning when the people came back, Ann raised the off-white awning with the yellow trim to unveil the masterpiece.

The wall Ann designed was shaped like a heart and stood prominently between the waterspout and the hospital. Ann positioned it perfectly so as to create a mystifying optical illusion from almost every angle in the park.

By using a rhythmic programming sequence, the water flowing over the wall made the heart appear to come alive at random times throughout the day. In addition to giving the children a fun way to cool off on hot days, the entertaining display renewed the parents' sense of hope by encouraging them to expect the unexpected. One of the unexpected things was the way the Sun cast Rooty's shadow upon the wall late in the morning. When the wind blew, causing her shadow to shift, it added to the pulsing effect of the wall and left Rooty feeling as if she and Wally had been reunited.

Danny reinforced this message by sitting beside the fountain and saying, "None of us can predict when the water will re-surface, bringing this heart of stone alive. Likewise we must remain faithful, for we never know when a miracle cure might surface for our children." Upon hearing him repeat this over and over again, some people just assumed the blind teacher was losing his mind.

Not surprisingly, all the fuss over whether the heart-shaped wall would be able to capture the image eventually divided the townspeople into the same familiar groups as before—believers and non-believers. The shop owner was under the impression that the number of non-believers was rising quickly.

When on several separate occasions the teenagers pointed out the image as it was banking off the building, passing through the water, and casting itself onto the brick wall, the non-believers response was predictable. "That's nothing more and nothing less than a normal rainbow. Read your fourth grade science book. Anytime light passes through water, it creates a rainbow." The woman who made this statement sounded very smart, but the frown on her face indicated she wasn't very happy.

For those who did believe in the miracles of Jelly Donut Junction, it didn't take long for Wally's memorial to become the most desired place in town to capture a photo opportunity; especially for those parents who weren't sure how much longer their sick children would be with them.

Rooty could see that many of the children were very sick like Wally had been before he was condemned. She overheard one young couple wrestling with the reality surrounding their daughter's deteriorating condition. "The doctors don't know if she will recover or not. All we can do now is pray." As they bowed their heads, Rooty, whose heart was breaking over their sad news, joined them in prayer. *Please help her recover. She's just an innocent child.*

○ ○ ○

Despite all the things going right in Rooty's life—like growing closer to the Sun than she ever dreamed possible; having great friends like Woody, Sammy, and Fluff supporting her; learning that Knotty was alive; and becoming the centerpiece of an alluring fountain—two things held Rooty back from being completely joy-filled and celebrating life to the fullest: She missed Wally and she longed to experience the touch of a child.

She was reminded how much she missed Wally every time she looked at the heart-shaped brick wall and of her desire to connect with the children every time an adult cut one of them off, preventing the child from playing in the pool surrounding her. She was reflecting on her problems when the Sun broke through the clouds and said, "Want to talk about it?"

Rooty, convinced the Sun knew her every thought anyway, welcomed the invitation. She decided it was time she laid it all on the line. "Yeah, I want to talk about it. I've wanted to talk about it ever since it happened, and you know it."

"Don't blame it on me, Rooty," replied the Sun.

"Then who should I blame it on? Remember, you're the Sun. Everything revolves around you, right?"

There was an edge to Rooty's voice that surprised even her, but she couldn't keep pretending that everything was all right between them. She needed an answer, and she needed it now. So she asked the Sun, "Why did you condemn Wally? He was a good building. He didn't do anything wrong. He believed in you. He loved you!"

"You can blame it on my Father, if that's what you choose to do, because I tell you the truth: The Sun can do nothing by himself. He can do only

> Then who should I blame it on?

what he sees his Father doing, because whatever the Father does the Sun also does."

Rooty was dumbfounded. She didn't know what to think or how to respond, but she knew one thing for sure—the Sun was reading her every thought. He confirmed this when he continued by saying, "Do not be amazed by this, Rooty. Do not continue thinking that Wally was condemned. He was not, because as you have just said, he believed in me. Not only did he believe in me, he believed in my father too."

Rooty remained speechless as she listened to the Sun. "And again, I tell you the truth, Rooty: Whoever hears my words and believes in him who sent me has eternal life and will not be condemned; he has crossed over from death to life. Now it is your turn to believe me when I tell you that my Father and I love Wally. That's why we saved him and invited him to come live with us for eternity."

Rooty was getting more and more confused. She didn't understand anything the Sun was saying, so she asked, "Who is your Father? Why haven't I ever seen him?"

"You have seen him, Rooty. When you look at me, you see the one who sent me," responded the Sun in a reassuring voice.

"The One who sent you? Now you've definitely lost me. I thought you were the center of the universe, and the earth and all of us on it revolved around you."

"I know it's hard to understand, Rooty, but everything does revolve around me. That's what I was trying to share with you earlier," he whispered his statement again, more slowly this time, giving Rooty a moment to reflect upon it in her heart. *The Sun can do nothing by himself, and apart from me you can do nothing of lasting value either.*

When he sensed she was ready to continue he added, "In other words, Rooty, we are all in this together. My Father has assigned each of us a unique role in *The Story.* As you already know, each of us, including me, was created to play a supporting role. That's where the term *history* comes from, Rooty. It's His story, my Father's story, the source from which all other stories find their meaning."

Rooty and the Sun continued to talk late into the afternoon. The Sun explained why his Father positioned him over all the world; why he charged him with drawing everyone and everything closer to himself; why he sent him to model forgiveness and mercy for the whole world to see.

Just before the Sun disappeared beyond the horizon Rooty shouted out, "Wait a minute. What about my other problem?"

"It's no problem at all. Just remember this: Faith is being sure of what we hope for and certain of what we do not see. In other words, keep the faith, Rooty. Keep asking questions, keep true to what you believe in, and most importantly keep praying for the children to come to you. The reason that is always on your mind is because my Father placed it in your heart. In fact, that's the very reason my Father had you placed at the center of the fountain to begin with."

○ ○ ○

Rooty never saw the world the same way after that day. Day in and day out she kept the eyes of her heart fixed on growing closer to the Sun. She learned to rely on him to care for her needs, regardless of what was happening in the surrounding scene. She did everything she could to remain rooted in faith. "Ever upward and onward" became her mantra after she overheard a woman saying it to one of her grandchildren as she struggled to climb up the slide. It had a catchy ring to it, so she started using it.

For several years she prayed the same prayer over and over again, relentlessly, expectantly: *Let the children come to me. Let the children come to me.*

Then one day, with some help from his older sister, a small boy, who had recently lost his eyesight, stepped off the wall and into the pool surrounding Rooty. His sister joined him. The cool water provided a welcome break from the heat. Within seconds the splashing began and their laughter captured the attention of every child and parent in the park. Some of the adults, seeing how much fun the two siblings were having, encouraged their kids to join in on the fun.

Unfortunately for the original two bathers, their mother was not one of those parents. When she looked up and saw what her kids had started, she was totally embarrassed. Her biggest concern was that the other parents would think she wasn't a good mother. She raced over to the edge of the pool, pulled the boy into the safety of her arms, and scolded her daughter, "What were you thinking, young lady? How dare you—"

"Sissy, throw me that red ball floating next to you!" shouted the boy.

His stunned mother took one look at the red ball floating in front of her daughter and broke into tears of joy. "What color is my shirt?" she asked.

"Blue with yellow butterflies," he replied without hesitating. The smile on his face was bigger than life.

"It's a miracle! My son can see again! I can't believe he can see again."

She picked up her son, nearly squeezing the insides out of him, and carried him into the fountain. There, alongside her daughter, the three of them celebrated life like they had never celebrated it before. Their enthusiasm was contagious. It spread like wildfire as more adults joined their kids in the pool. Likewise, the miracles spread as well.

The boy was not the only one healed that day, nor was he the only one to regain his vision. Rooty, who had been wondering if her faith would ever pay off, felt like she had truly caught a glimpse of heaven. The children were not only splashing in the pool, they were hugging her trunk.

Like Woody and Wally had years ago, Rooty had finally experienced the energizing power of a child's touch. The only thing she could compare it to was the first time she saw the Sun. Both instances had been worth the wait. When she looked into the children's eyes, their sense of hope, their deep faith, and their unconditional love inspired her. The entire experience renewed her faith, affirmed her role in *The Story,* and made her feel an unexplainable sense of connectedness to something bigger. Although she still missed Wally, she couldn't imagine being any more joy-filled than she was in that moment.

○ ○ ○

Before long, word of the healing water circulated beyond Jelly Donut Junction and people started flocking back to the small town again. When the crowds became too large and unruly for people to gather safely around the fountain, the mayor called a town meeting.

After listening to all kinds of crazy ideas on how to best handle the situation—ranging from charging admission to the park to restricting usage to hospital patients only—Danny spoke boldly.

"It's not the water that is healing the children," Danny announced to the crowd.

"Then what is it?" snapped a man whose son had recently been healed. "How do you explain the fact that Johnny can walk after entering the fountain?"

"It's easy to explain. Johnny has faith, and his faith has healed him. You have to have faith like a little child if you want to be healed."

Danny's statement rubbed many of the adults the wrong way, sparking a heated debate. To no one's surprise, the believers and non-believers took their respective sides again.

While they rehashed their tired old arguments, a teenager with a wonder-filled look on his face and an open mind asked Danny, "Are you saying only little children can be healed in this fountain?"

"Not exactly," replied Danny. Before he could complete his thought, a passionate group of believers, including the donut man and Artie, rushed to his aid. Several testified as to having been healed of their chronic ailments after stepping into the pool. Yet, when challenged by the non-believers in the crowd, none of them could produce the physical evidence necessary to support their claim.

Recognizing it was time to stop *telling* and to start *showing* the people the truth, Danny invited the crowd to follow him over to the fountain. Once they were all gathered around the pool, things only got worse. Several additional non-believers stepped forward claiming, "We've all tested the water ourselves without any success."

One man, who claimed to have been suffering from arthritis for years, stuck his hand in the water just to prove the non-believer's point. "See, nothing happens. My hand is just as stiff as ever," he scoffed. "Actually, for the first time in my life, I agree with the blind teacher. This water can't heal anybody," he cackled. "It certainly hasn't healed me."

Rather than wasting energy defending his point, Danny kindly replied, "You are right, my brother. This is the first time we have agreed. I only hope it will not be the last—for your sake."

With that Danny turned his attention back to the crowd. He instructed those closest to the pool, some who believed and some who didn't, to look into the water.

While they were looking into the pool he said to them, "I've brought you here to show you something important, something each of you is capable of seeing, should you choose to. I've brought you here to demonstrate how faith works; how faith is a choice, a choice that only you can make—ultimately it's the only choice you can make to truly live *the good life*."

After pausing to let his last comment sink in, Danny asked them, "What do you see?"

"Myself," responded one of the non-believers sarcastically.

"Excellent. How much of yourself can you see?" asked Danny.

"Only my face," he replied.

"Exactly. Now let me ask you this: What do you think I would see if I looked into the fountain?"

Danny's awkward question was met with an awkward silence. Assuming it was some kind of trick, the non-believers, not wanting to fall into his trap, chose to remain silent. The believers, although eager to help, didn't really understand what he was driving at either.

Danny stuck his cane in the water and used it like an eggbeater to stir the shallow pool. After waiting a moment to make sure the surface of the pool had been sufficiently disturbed, he instructed them to look into the fountain again before asking, "Now what do you see?"

"Nothing!" blurted out the same man who had replied to the first question.

"Interesting," said Danny as he opened *The Good Book*. After running his fingers along several pages, he found what he was seeking and read it to the crowd, "As water reflects a face, so a man's heart reflects a man."

How much of yourself can you see?

Turning away from where the man was standing, so as not to provoke him any further, he said, "The first time I asked all of you to look into the fountain, you expected to see your faces. But the second time, because I was making waves, none of you expected to see anything, did you? I'll bet some of you were so convinced that you wouldn't see anything that you didn't even look into the fountain. Am I right?"

After several people, including a few of the so-called believers, acknowledged that Danny was in fact right, he continued the lesson. "You didn't look because, based upon your past experience, you didn't believe you could see your reflection unless the water was perfectly calm. But unlike you, children, due to their natural sense of wonder, would not only look into the water the second time, they would expect to see their reflection again. Even though they wouldn't see it at first, they would keep on looking, believing that eventually their reflection would reappear."

"That's because they don't know any better," blurted out an older lady.

In this case it appears that ignorance is bliss, Danny thought to himself. Without skipping a beat he asked, "Does anyone remember what I've said in the past about one of the benefits of being blind?"

Carl was the first to respond, "Sure. You said, 'It's easier for the blind to see because they're not blinded by appearances.'"

"That's exactly the reason why it wouldn't make any difference whatsoever whether the water was calm or stirred, still or wavy, when I looked into the fountain. I would neither be distracted by the waves or be dependent upon the calm surface to see the reflection of who I am on the inside. Like the children, what I expect to see, what I believe in advance I will see, is not altered by the scene, because it is not a matter of the mind, it's a matter of the heart."

The believers in the crowd looked on approvingly as Danny continued his lesson. "In the same way, the children know it's not the water that makes the difference. In fact, they know it has nothing to do with anything on the outside, and everything to do with what they believe deep down inside their hearts."

"Danny, are you saying that when it comes to living the good life and to being healed—*what's inside matters?*" asked a young man as he pointed toward the message on the sign. "And that what's inside is based not upon what we can see, but upon what we can't see? Are you saying that everything in life comes down to what we believe, or don't believe—that it all comes down to faith?"

"I've never said it quite as well as you just did, but yes, that's exactly what I believe. Said differently, faith is believing in advance that which will only appear logical when viewed in reverse. Therefore, whether you simply want to see your reflection in a pool of water or hope to see the image when it appears next, you have to believe you will see it before you can see it. Unfortunately, if you choose to wait until you can see the image before you believe in the miracle itself, you will never see it. You can't wait until you do see it to believe it. Faith just doesn't work that way. It calls us to look beyond the scene to the unseen, to trust that things aren't always as they appear. Faith calls us to look at life through the expectant eyes of a little child."

○ ○ ○

The next morning, and every morning thereafter, a small group of believers, including Artie, Danny, and the donut man, stood watch near the fountain. On most days, the wind didn't blow hard enough to generate the enchanting music. Likewise, for whatever reason, the image did not always appear. That didn't stop them from expecting to see it nor from believing that it existed.

Artie saw the image often, perhaps more frequently than anyone else. That's because he spent his days next to the fountain airbrushing caricatures of those visiting the park. No matter how often he saw the image, it never looked the same twice.

Rooty grew very fond of Artie. She loved the way he looked up at her every time they were alone in the park. She could always tell when the image appeared by the look on his face. She vividly remembered his reaction on the eleventh day of the seventh month of the year, five years after the image had first been unveiled. It stuck out in her mind.

On that day, several hours after seeing the image, Artie came running over to Danny, who was telling his favorite story of the farmer sowing the seeds to a group of children in the park. Artie claimed to have seen a new message. After Danny finished his lesson and the children had gone, he asked his brother, "What did you see this time?"

In exactly the same manner as before, Artie guided Danny's hand, helping him trace the symbols in the sand.

ζητέω ἀλλά ἔσω

Unlike the previous time, however, Danny did not appear to be able to decipher the code. He didn't whisper anything in Artie's ear, nor did Artie jump up and run off like he had the first time around. In fact, as far as Rooty could tell, Artie never discovered the meaning of the second message. If he did, he locked it away, deep inside his heart, like hidden treasure.

Hundreds of believers continued to bring their sick children to play in the pool surrounding Rooty. They knew it wasn't the water that was healing the children. They understood it was their faith, but they loved listening to the blind teacher sing songs, spin tales, and share simple truths about life. And they enjoyed sitting underneath the majestic palm tree while dangling their toes in the cool water.

Rooty loved being at the center of the fountain. Not because she sought the attention, but because it afforded her the best platform from which to live out her role in *The Story*. It was a role she hadn't asked for and a role she wouldn't have traded for anything in the world.

Over the years, the image and the enchanting music reappeared often. Rooty overheard Artie telling a group of tourists that he was charting the appearances to see if there was a pattern. To her knowledge he never found one.

Rooty, Woody, and Knotty remain the best of friends to this very day. Each of them is still standing firmly in their assigned position, united in a common purpose—faithful to their quest to grow closer to the Sun and to each other.

One day, a few years after the donut man and Danny had gone on to rest in heaven, a group of grateful parents unveiled a sign of their own. It was etched into a large piece of granite and placed next to Wally's memorial.

In memory of our faithful guide, Danny, who lost his sight but never lost his eternal vision. Thanks for teaching us that things aren't always as they appear and for encouraging us to find our role in The Story.

The Quest Continues

Matty remained frozen in place until his grandfather finished sharing *The Story*. Traces of powdered sugar lingered in the corners of his mouth. His jelly-coated index finger was stuck to his milk glass.

Matty stared at the heart-shaped tattoo on his grandfather's forearm before blurting out, "Poppa, you were the young man in the red pickup truck! That story is all about you, isn't it?"

"Yes and no, Matty Boy. Yes, I was the one in the truck, but no, it's definitely not about me. In fact, *The Story* isn't about Rooty, Woody, or Uncle Danny either, although each of us played an important role in it."

"Uncle Danny? He was my uncle?" interrupted Matty.

"Sure was, your great uncle—and he sure was great." Poppa couldn't help but smile as he thought about his older brother. He missed him. Life in Jelly Donut Junction hadn't been the same since Danny passed away.

Poppa took a moment to review the cast for Matty. He explained how his father was the donut man. He noted how he'd opened the donut shop as a platform for ministry, a place in which people could gather to share *The Story*. And he talked about the vital role his father played in encouraging Danny to overcome his physical blindness; how he'd taught him to develop the eyes of his heart. Then, as hard as it was to share, Poppa told Matty how his father and Danny had both gone to heaven a few months before he came into the world.

"You see, Matty Boy, that's why their pictures are by the register. I hung them there the day before I sold the donut shop to one of my father's best friends. Others thought I was making a big mistake. They said, 'This place is a gold mine,' but I knew making donuts wasn't my role in *The Story*. So, even though it was the hardest thing I've ever had to do, I handed over the keys to the shop and left Jelly Donut Junction. At the time I thought I'd never return, but you know the rest of the story. We moved to the Midwest to be closer to you and your parents—"

"And then we all moved down here before I started Kindergarten," Matty interjected.

"Exactly, little man." Poppa glanced at his watch. He had time to cover one last thing.

"Danny was the best big brother ever. I'll never forget the day my father, your great grandfather, asked him to share *The Story* with me in this very booth." The old man looked over to make sure his grandson was still tracking with him before adding, "That was the day my quest began. I was about your age at the time."

"Almost six?"

"Yep, almost six," responded Poppa as he reached over and gently cleaned Matty Boy's hands and face.

"Well, are you ready for your quest to continue?" asked Poppa as he slid out of the booth.

Several tears rolled down the old man's cheeks as the words left his mouth. This time, he made no effort to conceal them or to limit their number. He knew that days like this were few and far between. Experience had taught him to soak up and cherish each new moment.

Although their day had already been chock full of incredible moments, the old man tingled with anticipation as he held his grandson's hand and led him toward the door. Matty Boy was seconds away from experiencing his breakthrough moment. That's what his Uncle Danny used to call the inside-out transition—when a person went from hearing *The Story* inside the shop to wanting to find their role in it outside of the shop.

The moment Matty stepped through the door he turned sharply to his right, hoping to see the Sun. Although he had seen the Sun many times before, this morning his desire to see him was stronger than usual. Something was different. Matty couldn't see the Sun, yet he could feel his presence. He could see the light breaking through the spaces between the tall buildings.

The old man led his grandson through the parking lot, across the street, and around the perimeter of the park. Along the way, Matty was quick to point out Woody, Banks, the old barber shop, the heart-shaped wall, and finally the children's hospital. Everything looked exactly as Matty had imagined when his grandfather was telling *The Story*. Everything, that is, except for the young girl waving to him from the window on the third floor of the hospital. She was new.

Matty didn't remember Poppa mentioning her. He wondered about *her role in The Story* as he waved back. The girl flashed the friendliest, happiest smile the boy had ever seen. What made her expression even more memorable was the fact that Matty didn't expect to see a sick kid smiling that way.

"Poppa, do you see that girl in the window?" asked Matty.

"Sure."

"Those kids in the hospital are really, really sick, right?"

"Right."

"Then why is she smiling like that?"

The old man marveled at the wisdom his grandson was displaying at such a young age. It was now obvious to him that Matty's quest was well underway. "She's smiling like that because she's already found her hidden treasure. Even though she's very sick, the treasure in her heart gives her the strength to smile."

For the next few minutes, they sat in silence while Matty processed his grandfather's response. He maintained eye contact with the girl in the window the entire time. His mind captured snapshots of her face and sent them to his heart to be developed. Her joyful smile made an indelible impression on him—one that inspired him to want to seek the hidden treasure all the more.

The old man paused for a moment to get his bearings. He wanted to make sure he was standing in the right place because the right time was quickly approaching.

Just then a squadron of pelicans flew by in tight formation, soaring freely upon the ocean breeze; the pair cocked their heads back in unison to watch them. After the pelicans disappeared, the old man noticed a change in Matty's mood. His grandson's smile had faded, his shoulders drooped.

"What's wrong, little man?"

"Rooty's gone. That's what's wrong! And I really wanted to see her. What happened to her, Poppa?"

"Now we don't know that for sure, Matty. Don't jump to conclusions. In a moment we'll walk over to the center of the park and look for her, okay?" said Poppa in a gentle voice.

The truth was, Poppa didn't know if Rooty was still there or not. *I sure hope she is. I'd love to see her again myself.*

Hoping to get Matty's mind off of Rooty for a moment, and to maintain their position between Banks and the heart-shaped wall, Poppa suggested they play a game.

"What kind of game?" asked Matty, his interest peaked.

"It's called the listening game," replied the old man. "Uncle Danny used to play it with the sick children from the hospital in this very spot. Here's how it works. We close our eyes, listen closely, and whoever names the most different sounds wins. Got it?"

Matty closed his eyes and began rifling off a variety of sounds. "The ocean, the water in the fountain, a seagull, a car—"

"Keep your list in your head, Matty, otherwise it's too hard for us to hear everything," whispered Poppa.

Matty did as he was asked.

They stood silently. The sound of the water cascading

toward them before it disappeared underneath the road provided a peaceful backdrop, the perfect setting for Poppa and Matty Boy to ponder the desires of their hearts.

Before long, Matty broke the silence. "Poppa, can I open my eyes now? Please!"

"Be patient, Matty. Some things in life are worth waiting for, and this is definitely one of those things. I know it's not easy to be still and wait, but sometimes it's the best thing to do. Don't forget, I've got my eyes closed, too. We're in this thing together, okay?"

Both of them listened intently for another minute. Matty was trying his hardest not to talk, but he had something important to share with his grandfather.

"Poppa, I think I can hear better with my eyes closed than I can when they are open. I think I can even hear your heart beating."

His comment choked up the old man, muffling his response. "Matty, we all hear much better with our eyes closed than we do with them open. That's why Uncle Danny used to say that 'the blind see below the surface better, they see what's inside more clearly—because they aren't blinded by appearances.'"

The wind was growing stronger. So was the old man's desire for the next few minutes to play out the way he'd dreamed they would. Now he was the one who was getting impatient. He couldn't wait to discover if his grandson was truly listening with his heart or just hearing with his head. He didn't have to wait long before he got his answer.

"Poppa, do you hear that?"

A huge gust of wind had burst onto the scene, which

was very unusual given there were no storms in the area. And with it came the enchanting music. It was faint at first, barely audible, but soon it filled the air. The sound of the music was out of this world. There was nothing Matty could compare it to. It was unlike anything he had ever heard. The music entered his ears and made a beeline straight for his heart.

Rather than responding to Matty's question out loud, the old man placed his right hand on the boy's shoulder and squeezed gently. Then he placed his left over the boy's eyes as a reminder to keep them closed—for he knew this would further enhance his grandson's experience.

As the wind died down, the music faded.

Poppa checked his watch. Then he removed his hand from his grandson's face. "You can open your eyes now, Matty Boy."

They were less than a minute away from the moment the old man had been waiting to experience with his grandson since the day he was born. Like clockwork, at precisely 7:11 a.m., the sunlight burst through Woody's holes and reflected off Banks, using him like a giant magnifying glass. Banks then deflected the intense light beam right over their heads toward the water spout. They both spun to see where it was heading. When the light passed through the water, it cast the image onto the heart-shaped brick wall. It was a spectacular vision, far exceeding the old man's wildest expectation and recollection.

"Poppa, do you see that!"

"Awesome!" replied the old man.

For the third time that morning, the world seemed to

stop spinning. Poppa and Matty were spellbound. Neither could move. Neither dared to speak another word, fearing they would somehow ruin the moment. The image was breathtaking. From where they stood, the wall appeared to be on fire. In the same way, it felt like their hearts were ablaze inside their chests.

The image remained slightly longer than it had in the past. Finally, a cloud passed in front of the Sun, ending the dazzling display. Matty looked up and wondered, *Could that be Fluff?*

After watching a few more clouds pass by, Matty's eyes shifted back to ground level. He scanned the scene, looking to the left and then to the right. Then he looked back toward the hospital to see if the sick little girl in the window had seen it too. She had. Matty could tell because her smile was even bigger. Matty started clapping his hands above his head and jumping up and down. He just felt like celebrating. When he did, the little girl followed his lead.

Having cheered with his new friend, he shot her a wave and turned his attention back to the rest of the scene. Within seconds, he realized that he, his grandfather, and his new friend were the only three that had seen the image. That disturbed him deeply, causing him to ask, "Poppa, why didn't anyone else come here today?"

"That's a great question, Matty, but it's kind of a hard one to answer."

The disappointment in Matty's eyes convinced him to try anyway. "Matty, do you remember the story Uncle Danny read to the children about the farmer sewing the seeds?"

Matty nodded.

"Well, it works the same way with people. Some people don't believe they're on a quest. In other words, they don't believe they were ever part of *The Story* to begin with. Therefore, they don't expect to see the image or to hear the enchanting music. They close their minds and limit the possibilities of what they can see and what they can hear. When they do, they lose their childlike sense of wonder and overlook the miracles occurring right before their eyes."

"That's kind of like what happened when Uncle Danny asked the people to look into the fountain after he stirred the water with his cane, right?" interjected Matty.

Matty's comment caught the old man completely off guard. *Perhaps he understands more than I think he does.*

"That's exactly right, Matty Boy. Some live their entire lives like the seeds on the path. Others get too busy, too easily distracted, to continue their quest. They are like the seeds sown in the thorns. Still others start their quest but eventually turn back because things don't work out exactly the way they planned for them to. Then, there are those who abandon their quest altogether, thinking the effort required isn't worth it in the end. I guess you could say their hope of finding the hidden treasure is dashed on the rocks like the seed the farmer scattered on the rocky ground."

"How come you never aband…aban…gave up, Poppa?" asked Matty.

"Oh, there are lots of reasons, Matty, but the biggest reason is that my father and your Uncle Danny made sure that my seeds were planted in good soil. Like Rooty, they invested their lives in mine and stayed close by my side until my faith took root." Poppa paused for a moment. Matty's question unlocked an important lesson that he'd overlooked until now.

"Matty Boy, my father and Danny did one other thing that was really important. They taught me not to act like Knotty. They explained the dangers of trying to prove that I could stand on my own. They encouraged me to be like Rooty. Don't get me wrong, there were times when I tried to prove myself to others, to show how fast, how smart, or how daring I was. Fortunately, Uncle Danny and my father were always close by, reminding me to embrace my lifelines—to spend time reading *The Good Book* everyday. Looking back now, Matty Boy, that's what got me through the windy and stormy times in my life."

"Hey, Poppa, my mom and dad read me stories from *The Good Book* all the time. Does that mean I'm rooted in good soil too?"

The old man couldn't be any prouder of his grandson. "You betcha! You're definitely rooted in good soil."

The talk about roots and good soil brought Matty full circle. With an uneasy look on his face, he asked his Poppa, "Can we look for Rooty now? You promised!"

"Sure, but close your eyes. It will be more fun that way." The old man led Matty slowly over toward the circular pool.

The closer they got the more clearly Matty could hear the sound of the water entering the pool. Poppa stopped right next to the wall separating the fountain from the rest of the park. Now Matty heard the sound he was seeking; the sound of palm branches brushing against each other. He tilted his head back and opened his eyes. Then he flopped to the ground and began to whine.

"She's gone, Poppa. Rooty's gone. I knew it."

The look of disappointment on his grandson's face nearly broke the old man's heart.

"Matty, never forget that things aren't always as they appear. The scene—what we can physically see—too often masks the unseen truth about life. Sometimes we have to stop, look, and listen more closely before we find the things we are searching for in life. Oftentimes, we need to be more patient if we want to see things more clearly. Now, look more closely. Rooty is here. She just doesn't look exactly the way you expect her to."

The boy looked up again. Prior to that moment, he hadn't noticed the enormous tree looming over them. He'd been so focused on looking at the familiar parts of the scene he somehow managed to overlook the most amazing tree he had ever seen. Its trunk was massive, and its roots stretched beyond the walls of the pool. The branches formed a canopy over the entire park. *This must be the biggest tree in the whole wide world,* he thought to himself.

"Poppa, I thought Rooty was supposed to be at the center of the fountain?" Matty glared up at the big tree, visibly upset with it.

The old man, reading his grandson's expression said, "Remember, things aren't always as they appear. I know it looks like this big, old tree stole Rooty's role in the spotlight, but that's truly not the case. What really happened was Uncle Danny and the Tree Doctor called upon Rooty to play a bigger role in *The Story*—the role of a host tree."

"What does a host tree do, Poppa?"

"A host tree dedicates its life to helping another tree establish its roots. By burying the seeds in Rooty's trunk, the tree doctor knew they would receive the protection, water, and exposure to the sun they needed to grow stronger roots faster. In a way, Rooty acted like this giant tree's mother, lending him her roots until this grand old tree's roots had enough time to sink deeply into the good soil."

"What happened to Rooty after that?"

"Over the years, she faded farther and farther from sight, but grew closer and closer to the Sun. The farther she faded, the more she felt like she was fulfilling her unique role in *The Story*. And the more she felt this way, the more joy she experienced."

Poppa paused to soak up the look on Matty's face. His jaw was gaping and his pupils were fully dilated. Poppa could practically hear Matty thinking. He definitely had Matty's undivided attention. Knowing that, he decided to ratchet up the lesson a notch or two.

"I remember Uncle Danny used to refer to Rooty whenever he was teaching the children about life. He used to say, 'Not all of us are called to become a centerpiece, like this grand old tree, but all of us are expected to play a supporting role in *The Story*. Some of us will be asked to plant the seeds, others to water them, and still others simply to encourage them to grow closer to the Sun each day.'"

"Poppa, how do we find our role?" asked Matty.

"Uncle Danny used to answer that question this way. 'We don't find our role, our role finds us—but only if we make the time to listen to the still, small voice buried deep inside our hearts.'"

"How does my role find me?"

"Matty, your role in *The Story* will find you exactly the same way your role in last year's school play found you— you will be cast into it.

The boy reflected back. *Being the lead elf, the chief toymaker, sure was a lot of fun.*

Poppa could see that he was lost in thought, so he waited for a moment. "Matty Boy, life works exactly the same way. We're all cast into a particular role, based upon our unique talents and gifts. At first, some of us consider casting our roles away. This happens for a variety of reasons, but typically it's because we don't think our roles are interesting enough, important enough, big enough, or visible enough—or we think that it will be too hard for us to play. Others, like Rooty, obediently embrace whatever role they're assigned. They sacrifice their chance to stand out, preferring to stand on faith, instead of fame. Faithful characters trust that the author of *The Story* knows best. So they wait to see where their roles will lead them, knowing that in the end, all of us are simply playing a supporting role anyway."

The old man reached down, picked up his grandson, and raised him up into the crotch of the great tree. "Matty, perhaps if you look at the scene from a different angle, you'll be able to see Rooty and better appreciate the role she is playing."

Poppa's comment renewed the boy's hope. Matty grabbed hold of a branch and climbed up a few more feet before sitting down. He felt like a king looking over his kingdom as he continued listening to his grandfather.

"Matty, as you are about to see, Rooty is playing her role exactly the way it was cast. She's been standing firm, rooted in faith, living out her purpose for all these years. That's why what's inside of this grand old tree is the faithful heart of a palm."

The old man encouraged Matty to turn around and say hello to Rooty. He pointed out how the bark on her trunk was a different texture than the rest of the tree. Then he watched the boy's eyes follow her trunk upward. When Matty's eyes picked up Rooty's palm branches waving gracefully in the ocean breeze, he threw his arms around her trunk and squeezed.

After a while, when Matty had hugged until his little arms couldn't hug any more, he turned and reached down so his grandfather could help him out of the tree. No sooner did his feet hit the ground than he launched another question.

"Poppa, how did you and Uncle Danny get to be so smart?"

Poppa burst out laughing. *This kid is really something special,* he thought to himself.

After setting Matty down, he kneeled down facing him, placed his hands gently on his shoulders, and looked him straight in the eye. With a warm smile on his face he said, "Poppa's not smart; I'm experienced. And Uncle Danny was wise. There's a big difference, Matty Boy, between being smart and being wise. Being smart means you strive to have all the right answers. Being wise means you seek to ask all the right questions."

Matty's eyes had glazed over again. It was obvious that the old man's words were going right over his head. Knowing this, Poppa squeezed his grandson's shoulders gently and kept his main point simple. "Matty, without questions, there is no *quest*."

While Matty processed this last statement, the old man reflected on the vital life lesson his own father had shared with him and Danny a short time after the image first appeared. "*Boys, over the past fifty years, I've learned the key to continuing our quest. We need to spend more time listening to our hearts, not our heads. The best questions in life, the ones that help us stay on the right path, always flow from our hearts to our heads; not the other way around.*" The old man would have to wait until Matty was a little older before he could share this truth with him.

Matty didn't want his quest to end because he sensed something important was bubbling to the surface; working its way from his tummy to his head. But it wasn't a question just yet. *The symbols. The new ones.* He took a deep breath. *Uncle Danny.* It rattled around in his mind for a moment. *What do they mean?* Then he finally spit it out. "What did Uncle Danny whisper in your ear? What did the new symbols mean?"

Just when you think he's tapped out—Wham!—he comes out of nowhere with a doozie. "Uncle Danny never told me what the symbols meant."

"So, you figured it out yourself, Poppa?"

"Matty, the truth is I still don't know what the symbols

mean. But not a day has gone by since I first saw the image that I haven't wished I did." Now Poppa's expression was the one oozing disappointment.

Seeing the sad look on his Poppa's face really bothered Matty Boy. He grabbed his grandfather by the hand and dragged him across the street.

"Matty Boy, where are you taking me?" asked the old man.

"On a re-quest, Poppa."

As soon as they were safely across the street, Matty broke free and raced toward the sign.

The Re-Quest

When the old man caught up to his grandson, he found him sitting on the ground, a short distance from the truck. He was facing the large sign, but his eyes were closed.

"Now what are you doing, little man?" asked Poppa.

When Matty didn't respond, he assumed his grandson was getting tired, so he said, "Well, Matty Boy, now that you've found the hidden treasure, we best be getting home."

"We can't leave Jelly Donut Junction!" Matty's voice had an unexpected edge to it—a sense of urgency that surprised the old man. "We haven't figured out what the symbols mean yet."

Matty stuck his hand out with his index finger extended. "Poppa, will you draw the symbols for me, the same way you did with Uncle Danny?"

The old man was quick to honor his grandson's request. He placed his hand gently over his grandson's and, using Matty's tiny index finger, traced the first set in the sand, followed closely by the second.

$$\text{ἀλλά ἔσω λόγος}$$

$$\text{ζητέω ἀλλά ἔσω}$$

Matty's eyes fixated on the symbols. The old man watched as the wheels inside his grandson's head churned. The scene was familiar, but unique. Poppa waited patiently, thinking to himself, *After fifty years of searching for the meaning of the symbols, what's another few minutes going to hurt?*

Poppa figured the riddle would stump Matty Boy too, but it didn't. "Poppa, they look the same to me," he said offhand.

The old man was dumfounded, as he looked down at the symbols. He found it hard to draw a full breath. *He's right! It's been hidden in plain sight all this time. How could I have missed it?* Poppa shook his head in disbelief. *I know exactly how I missed it. I stopped looking at the symbols through the faithful eyes of a child.*

Over time the symbols had become so familiar, it never crossed his mind to compare the second set to the first; until now. Once he did, the unseen truth burst onto the scene.

With tears flooding his face, he picked Matty up and twirled him around. He squeezed his grandson so hard and spun him so fast that by the time they stopped, they were both disoriented. Matty loved it. Poppa felt a little queasy. But that didn't stop him for long.

The time had come to finish the quest he'd started over fifty years ago.

The next five minutes were a whirlwind of activity. In short order Poppa put Matty down, waited for his immediate world to stop spinning, retrieved his airbrush from the truck, and walked back toward Matty. The boy hadn't moved. He was still staring at the symbols etched in the sand.

"Poppa, did you figure out what the symbols mean?" asked Matty. "Tell me, Poppa, did you? Did you?"

"Nope, Matty Boy, I didn't," said the old man. Then, no longer able to contain himself, he blurted out. "But you did, Matty Boy! You cracked the code!"

Again, he grabbed the boy and spun him in a circle until he was too dizzy to spin him anymore. They flopped to the ground in a heap of joy. The old man's spirit was contagious; their laughter filled the air. Neither would ever forget this moment.

"Poppa, tell me what the symbols means. Tell me what they mean!" Matty pleaded.

"I'd rather show you. Follow me."

He led the boy up the stairway and onto the metal platform. Matty was about to touch one of the holes when Poppa handed him the airbrush. The old man placed his hand gently on top of the boy's. Then together, using the exact same lettering, they painted a new message right next the first.

While they painted, Poppa reflected upon his role in Jelly Donut Junction. Contrary to what others believed over the years, he hadn't made up the symbols. Nor had he deciphered them. The truth be told, the idea to write them on the sign wasn't even his. He was not the creator of the message. He was just the scribe—the one asked to share the message with others. That was his role in *The Story*. Nothing more, nothing less. It was a role he embraced; one for which he was eternally grateful.

When they were finished they made their way back down the stairs over toward where they had drawn the symbols in the sand. The old man, humbled by the role he'd been cast into, dropped to his knees, closed his eyes, and reflected on the way this day had begun.

The symbols.

What do they mean?

The moment this familiar question surfaced, he felt like the world stopped spinning again, just for a moment—as if he were standing on the edge of time, straddling the invisible boundary separating the past from the future. *It seems like only yesterday that I first laid eyes on the symbols, but it wasn't.*

Many days had come and gone. But none of them could compare to this day, the eleventh day of the seventh month of the year. For this was the day his grandson's quest got underway and his search for the meaning of the symbols came to an end. He had felt the gravity of their meaning since his youth, and now he finally knew what they meant.

What's inside matters, so seek what's inside.

Epilogue

The Story is unfolding.

If we look closely and listen carefully enough, this becomes clear. Each scene is in motion—filled with new sights and new sounds. And every moment is fresh; no two are alike. As amazing as this is, there is more.

You have a role! Here's the way to find it.

Ask and it will be given to you; seek and you will find; knock and the door will be opened to you. For everyone who asks receives; he who seeks finds; and to him who knocks, the door will be opened.

Therefore we do not lose heart. Though outwardly we are wasting away, yet inwardly we are being renewed day by day. For our light and momentary troubles are achieving for us an eternal glory that far outweighs them all. So we fix our eyes not on what is seen, but on what is unseen. For what is seen is temporary, but what is unseen is eternal.

Enjoy your quest…

Acknowledgments

First and foremost, I want to thank God. Apart from you, there is no quest, no hidden treasure—no story.

Now I'd like to thank my supporting cast members; those people who allow me to play my role in *The Story*. Heartfelt thanks to my wife, Debbie, for the gift of our five children, for being a great mom, and for taking on extra parenting duty during the writing of this book. Inexpressible thanks to my mom and dad for pouring your lives into mine. The seeds of your love have found good soil. Also, Dad, thanks for coming alongside me during the creation and editing phases of this manuscript. Your encouragement and insights were invaluable and greatly appreciated.

Additionally, I want to thank several people who played a direct and vital role in the creation of this book. Sarah Hughes, the young woman who asked, "What happens next?" igniting my quest to find this book hidden deep within my heart; Tim Morrison, my writing coach, who taught me how to write from my heart instead of my head and then poured his heart into the editing phase; James Earp, who introduced me to my publisher, Tate Publishing; the Tate family, for helping me bring *The Story* to life; Teresa Snider, for encouraging me to read between the lines;

John Puetz, for his loving reminders to keep writing; Dave Cook and Lloyd Reeb, two gifted life coaches who have influenced what's inside my heart greatly; all of my friends and colleagues at Wells Real Estate Funds, especially Doug Buce. Doug, you've inspired me to become a better husband, father, friend, and communicator. Thanks for believing in me and helping me find my role in *The Story*.

About the Author

Joe Colavito is an inspirational speaker and a business and life coach who enjoys connecting people with ideas. As the Vice President of External Development for Wells University, the educational arm of Wells Real Estate Funds, he leads a team dedicated to encouraging hundreds of financial advisors annually to find their role in *The Story*. His coaching philosophy focuses on helping others discover, develop, and deploy their God-given strengths to better serve their families, colleagues, and clients. Joe and his wife, Debbie, reside in Duluth, Georgia, with their five children: Jessie, Courtney, Andrea, Matthew, and Katie.